Preface

This book, *Cloud Computing: A Beginner's Guide to Expertise*, is designed to demystify cloud computing and provide a comprehensive introduction to this transformative technology. Whether you are a student, a professional looking to upskill, or simply someone curious about the cloud, this guide will take you from the basics to a deeper understanding of cloud architecture, services, and deployment models.

We begin with an overview of the fundamental concepts, including the definition of cloud computing, its history, and the key players in the industry. As we progress, you will learn about different cloud service models—Infrastructure as a Service (IaaS), Platform as a Service (PaaS), and Software as a Service (SaaS)—and how they can be leveraged to meet various business needs.

Practical examples and real-world case studies are included to help you see how cloud computing is applied in different industries. You will also find hands-on exercises to practice your skills and deepen your understanding. By the end of this book, you will not only have a solid grasp of cloud computing fundamentals but also be equipped with the knowledge to explore more advanced topics and certifications.

Table of Contents

Chapter 1: Introduction to Cloud Computing

Definition and History

Cloud computing refers to the delivery of computing services—including servers, storage, databases, networking, software, and more—over the internet ("the cloud") to offer faster innovation, flexible resources, and economies of scale. It typically operates on a pay-as-you-go or subscription-based model, allowing users to access resources on-demand without the need for significant upfront investment in hardware or infrastructure.

The history of cloud computing can be traced back to the 1950s, with the concept evolving over time alongside advancements in technology. However, it wasn't until the early 2000s that cloud computing began to gain significant traction with the emergence of internet-based services and the availability of high-speed internet connections.

One of the earliest manifestations of cloud computing was the development of grid computing, which involved the pooling of resources from multiple computers to solve complex problems. This concept laid the foundation for the modern cloud computing model.

Amazon Web Services (AWS) played a pivotal role in popularizing cloud computing with the launch of Amazon Elastic Compute Cloud (Amazon EC2) in 2006, which allowed users to rent virtual computers on which to run their applications. This marked the beginning of the era of Infrastructure as a Service (IaaS), where users could access computing resources over the internet.

Other major players in the cloud computing industry, such as Microsoft with Azure and Google with Google Cloud Platform, followed suit, offering their own cloud services and driving further innovation in the space.

Over time, cloud computing has evolved to encompass a wide range of services, including Platform as a Service (PaaS) and Software as a Service (SaaS), providing users with even greater flexibility and scalability in deploying and managing their applications and data. Today, cloud computing has become an essential component of the modern IT landscape, powering businesses of all sizes across various industries.

Evolution of Cloud Computing

The evolution of cloud computing has been marked by several key developments and shifts in technology, business models, and user expectations. Here's a breakdown of the major stages in the evolution of cloud computing:

Early Concepts (1950s-1990s): The roots of cloud computing can be traced back to the 1950s with the development of mainframe computing. Concepts such as utility computing and time-sharing laid the groundwork for sharing computing resources among multiple users. However, these early systems were limited by high costs and the lack of widespread internet connectivity.

Internet Era (1990s-2000s): The advent of the internet and advancements in networking technologies paved the way for the expansion of cloud computing. Companies began offering web-based services and applications accessible over the internet, leading to the emergence of Software as a Service (SaaS) models.

Grid Computing and Virtualization (2000s): Grid computing, which involved the pooling of resources from multiple computers to solve complex problems, provided an early model for distributed computing. Virtualization technologies allowed for the creation of virtual instances of hardware, enabling greater flexibility and efficiency in resource utilization.

Amazon Web Services (AWS) and Infrastructure as a Service (IaaS) (2006): The launch of Amazon Web Services (AWS) in 2006 with services like Amazon Elastic Compute Cloud (EC2) marked a significant milestone in the evolution of cloud computing. AWS popularized the concept of Infrastructure as a Service (IaaS), allowing users to rent virtualized computing resources on-demand over the internet.

Platform as a Service (PaaS) and Containers (2010s): Platform as a Service (PaaS) offerings, such as Google App Engine and Microsoft Azure, emerged to provide developers with tools and frameworks for building, deploying, and managing applications without worrying about underlying infrastructure. The rise of containerization technologies, led by Docker, Kubernetes, and others, further streamlined application deployment and management across different cloud environments.

Hybrid and Multi-Cloud (2010s-2020s): Organizations increasingly adopted hybrid and multi-cloud strategies to leverage the benefits of both public and private clouds while minimizing vendor lock-in and improving resilience. Cloud providers expanded their offerings to include more specialized services, such as artificial intelligence (AI), machine learning (ML), Internet of Things (IoT), and serverless computing.

Edge Computing and Beyond (2020s and Beyond): The proliferation of connected devices and the need for low-latency applications have driven interest in edge computing, which involves processing data closer to the source of generation. Cloud providers are expanding their infrastructure to the edge to support emerging use cases in industries such as IoT, autonomous vehicles, and telecommunications.

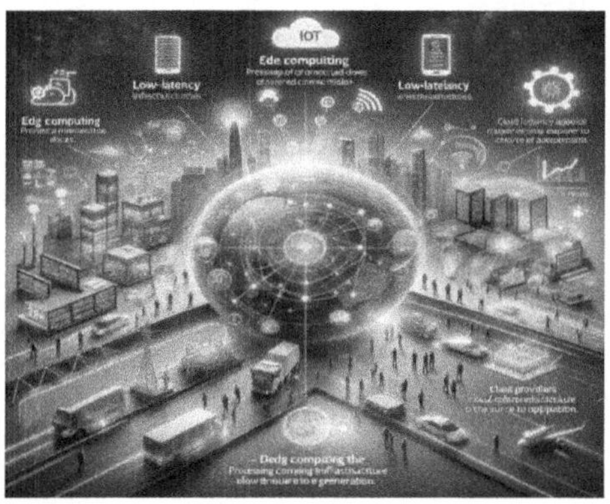

Overall, cloud computing continues to evolve rapidly, driven by advancements in technology, changing business needs, and shifting user expectations.

Characteristics of Cloud Computing (NIST)

The National Institute of Standards and Technology (NIST) outlines five essential characteristics of cloud computing:

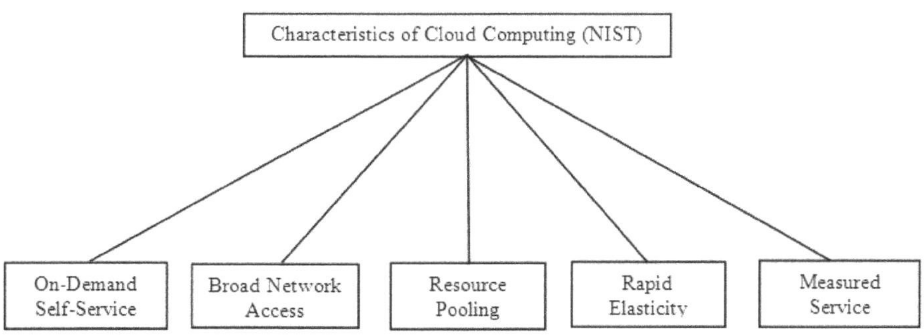

On-Demand Self-Service: Users can provision computing resources, such as server time and network storage, as needed without requiring human intervention from the service provider.

Broad Network Access: Cloud services are accessible over the network and can be accessed through standard mechanisms, promoting ubiquitous access from a variety of devices and platforms.

Resource Pooling: The provider's computing resources are pooled to serve multiple consumers using a multi-tenant model, with different physical and virtual resources dynamically assigned and reassigned according to consumer demand.

Rapid Elasticity: Cloud services can be rapidly scaled up or down to accommodate fluctuations in demand. Resources are automatically allocated and released, allowing for quick provisioning and de-provisioning of resources as needed.

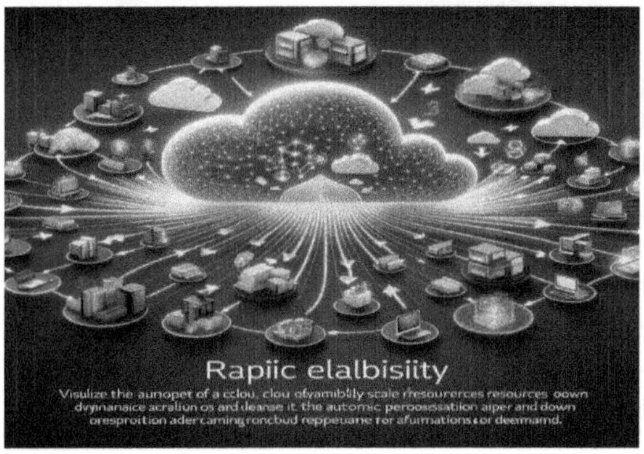

Measured Service: Cloud systems automatically control and optimize resource usage by leveraging a metering capability at some level of abstraction appropriate to the type of service (e.g., storage, processing, bandwidth, and active user accounts). Resource usage can be monitored, controlled, and reported, providing transparency for both the provider and consumer.

These characteristics collectively define the fundamental principles of cloud computing, enabling users to access computing resources on-demand, scale dynamically, and pay only for what they consume.

Usage Scenarios and Applications

Cloud computing has revolutionized various industry sectors by providing scalable, flexible, and efficient solutions. Here are some detailed examples of common usage scenarios and applications across different facets of cloud computing:

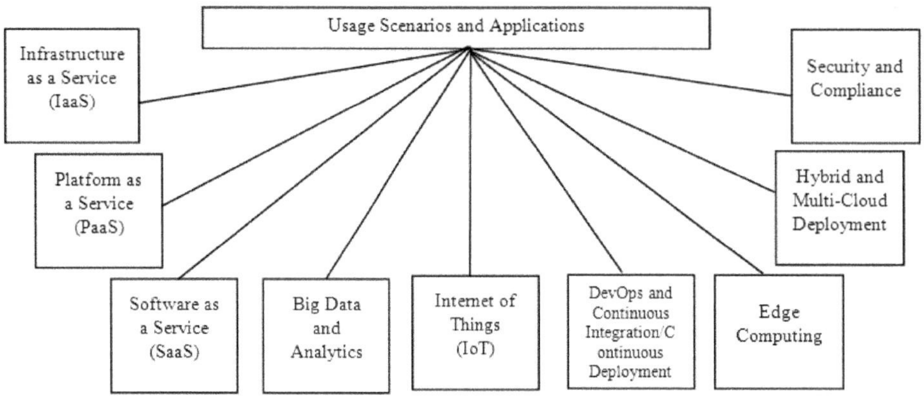

Infrastructure as a Service (IaaS)

Virtual Machines (VMs): Provisioning of VMs on-demand allows companies to set up development, testing, and production environments quickly and cost-effectively.

Storage: Businesses can utilize cloud storage for managing large volumes of data, including backups and disaster recovery solutions, ensuring data durability and accessibility.

Platform as a Service (PaaS)

Application Development: Developers can build, deploy, and scale applications rapidly without the complexity of managing servers, storage, and networking.

Database Services: Managed database services in the cloud offer scalability and high availability for data storage and management, simplifying database administration tasks.

Software as a Service (SaaS)

Productivity Tools: Cloud-based applications such as Microsoft 365 and Google Workspace enhance collaboration and productivity by providing tools for email, document sharing, and project management.

Customer Relationship Management (CRM): Platforms like Salesforce streamline customer management processes by offering robust CRM solutions that are accessible from anywhere.

Big Data and Analytics

Data Processing: Utilizing powerful cloud-based tools like Apache Hadoop and Spark to process and analyse large datasets efficiently.

Machine Learning: Platforms such as AWS Sage Maker and Google Cloud AI Platform support the training and deployment of machine learning models at scale, facilitating advanced data analysis and predictive modeling.

Internet of Things (IoT)

Data Collection and Analysis: Cloud computing enables the collection and analysis of data from IoT devices, supporting real-time decision-making and operational efficiencies.

DevOps and Continuous Integration/Continuous Deployment (CI/CD)

Automated Deployment: Cloud platforms facilitate the automation of the deployment pipeline, enhancing the speed and reliability of software releases.

Containerization: Services like Docker and Kubernetes help in building, deploying, and managing containerized applications, promoting microservices architectures.

Edge Computing

Low-Latency Applications: Running applications closer to end-users or IoT devices to minimize latency and enhance user experiences.

Offline Capabilities: Enabling data processing locally at the edge to provide offline functionalities and reduce dependencies on central servers.

Hybrid and Multi-Cloud Deployments

Disaster Recovery: Implementing strategies across multiple clouds to ensure business continuity and robust disaster recovery.

Optimizing Costs: Using diverse cloud providers to capitalize on cost efficiencies and minimize risks associated with vendor lock-in.

Security and Compliance

Identity and Access Management (IAM): Robust management of user identities and permissions in the cloud to ensure security and compliance.

Data Encryption: Ensuring the confidentiality and integrity of data with encryption techniques both at rest and in transit.

Content Delivery and Media Streaming

Content Delivery Networks (CDNs): Enhancing global content delivery with reduced latency, ensuring high availability and performance.

Live Video Streaming: Facilitating the broadcasting of live events and content to a wide audience over the internet, optimizing for scalability and quality.

These scenarios highlight the versatility and potential of cloud computing in adapting to various operational needs, driving innovation, and supporting the dynamic demands of modern businesses. As technology evolves, the scope of cloud computing continues to expand, unlocking new possibilities and applications.

Summary

Cloud Computing Overview: Cloud computing refers to the delivery of computing services over the internet, enabling faster innovation, flexible resources, and economies of scale, typically operating on a pay-as-you-go model.

History of Cloud Computing: The concept dates back to the 1950s, with significant advancements in the early 2000s, particularly with the introduction of Amazon Web Services (AWS) in 2006, marking the rise of Infrastructure as a Service (IaaS).

Evolution of Cloud Computing: Cloud computing has evolved through stages including early mainframe computing, the internet era, grid computing, the rise of virtualization, the emergence of PaaS and containers, hybrid and multi-cloud strategies, and edge computing.

NIST Characteristics of Cloud Computing: The essential characteristics include on-demand self-service, broad network access, resource pooling, rapid elasticity, and measured service, defining the principles that make cloud computing scalable, accessible, and efficient.

Usage Scenarios and Applications: Cloud computing is applied across various domains, including IaaS for virtual machines and storage, PaaS for application development, SaaS for productivity tools and CRM, big data and analytics, IoT, DevOps, edge computing, hybrid and multi-cloud deployments, security, and content delivery.

Glossary

Cloud Computing: The delivery of computing services such as servers, storage, databases, networking, and software over the internet, enabling faster innovation and flexible resources, often through a pay-as-you-go model.

Grid Computing: A form of distributed computing that involves pooling resources from multiple computers to solve complex problems, laying the foundation for modern cloud computing.

Infrastructure as a Service (IaaS): A cloud computing model where users can rent virtualized computing resources over the internet, providing flexibility and scalability without requiring significant upfront investment in hardware.

Platform as a Service (PaaS): A cloud service model that provides developers with tools and frameworks to build, deploy, and manage applications without managing the underlying infrastructure.

Software as a Service (SaaS): A cloud service model where software applications are delivered over the internet, allowing users to access and use them via a web browser without installing or managing the software themselves.

Virtualization: A technology that creates virtual instances of hardware, enabling more efficient use of resources by allowing multiple virtual machines to run on a single physical machine.

Amazon Web Services (AWS): A pioneer in cloud computing, AWS popularized the concept of IaaS with the launch of Amazon EC2 in 2006, allowing users to rent virtual computing resources on-demand.

NIST Characteristics of Cloud Computing: A set of five essential characteristics defined by the National Institute of Standards and Technology, including on-demand self-service, broad network access, resource pooling, rapid elasticity, and measured service.

Edge Computing: A computing paradigm that processes data closer to the data source, reducing latency and bandwidth usage, and supporting applications requiring real-time processing.

Hybrid and Multi-Cloud Deployments: Strategies that involve using multiple cloud providers or a combination of public and private clouds to leverage the benefits of each while minimizing risks like vendor lock-in.

Exercise

Exercise 1 – MCQ

1. Which of the following is NOT considered a key characteristic of cloud computing according to NIST?

a) On-Demand Self-Service

b) Measured Service

c) Multi-Tenancy

d) Rapid Elasticity

2. Which of the following is an example of a usage scenario for cloud computing?

a) Personal email hosting

b) Large-scale data analysis

c) Simple calculator app

d) Single-player offline games

Exercise 2 – True/ False

1. Cloud computing refers to the delivery of computing services over the internet.
2. The history of cloud computing dates back to the early 20th century.

Exercise 3 – Fill in the blanks

1. Cloud computing refers to the delivery of computing services over the ____________.
2. The National Institute of Standards and Technology (NIST) has defined ____________ essential characteristics of cloud computing.

Exercise 4 – One-Word

1. Who is often credited with popularizing the concept of cloud computing in the 2000s?
2. Which organization defined the essential characteristics of cloud computing?

Exercise 5 – Small answer

1. What is the National Institute of Standards and Technology (NIST) known for regarding cloud computing?
2. Can you briefly explain one of the key characteristics of cloud computing according to NIST?

Exercise 6 – Long answer

1. Discuss the evolution of cloud computing and its significance in the modern era of technology.

2. Provide examples and elaborate on different usage scenarios and applications of cloud computing in various industries.

Answer

Exercise 1 – MCQ

Ans: 1 c, 2 b.

Exercise 2 – True/False

Ans: 1 True, 2 False.

Exercise 3 – Fill in The Blanks

Ans: 1 Internet, 2 Five

Exercise 4 – One-Word

Ans: 1 Amazon, 2 NIST.

Online Resources

1. **True/False Practice Paper Link :** https://forms.gle/xnnd7Sg8fExdAEQPA

QR Code :

2. **True/False Video Link:** https://www.youtube.com/playlist?list=PLzlh_31VWEFr3Ge5hlmjFvfRvUnKrSIni

QR Code :

3. **One Word Practice Paper:** https://forms.gle/jaHV7nfrsxuRoFjX8

QR Code:

4. **One Word Video Link:**

https://www.youtube.com/playlist?list=PLzlh_31VWEFrrCrcdpNvnVnWqkrR6mt4R

QR Code:

Chapter 2: Cloud Architecture Models and Infrastructure

System Models for Distributed and Cloud Computing

In the realm of distributed and cloud computing, various system models have emerged to effectively manage and utilize resources across networks. These models serve as blueprints for organizing and structuring computing environments, facilitating efficient communication, resource allocation, and scalability.

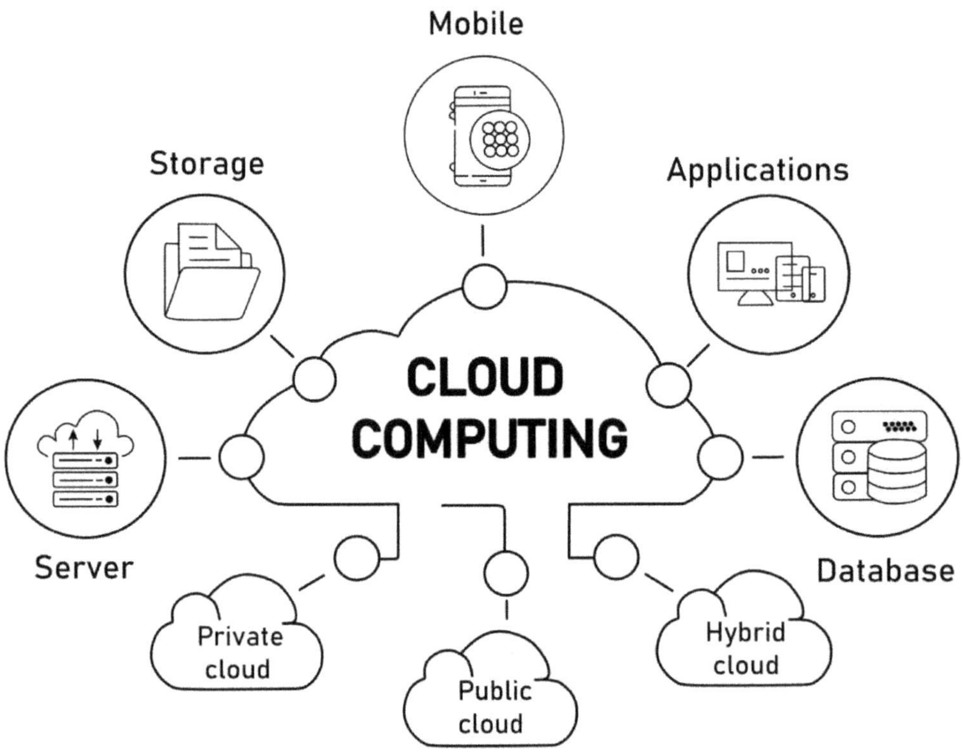

One prominent system model is the Client-Server architecture, where clients request services or resources from centralized servers. This model allows for centralized management and maintenance of data and applications, making it suitable for scenarios requiring reliable data storage and processing.

Another key model is Peer-to-Peer (P2P) architecture, where nodes in the network act both as clients and servers, collaborating to share resources directly. P2P systems excel in decentralized environments, promoting resource sharing and scalability without reliance on centralized infrastructure.

Additionally, the Service-Oriented Architecture (SOA) model focuses on organizing software components into services that can be accessed over a network. This approach emphasizes modularity, interoperability, and reusability, enabling flexible and agile development of distributed systems.

Cloud computing introduces further system models such as Infrastructure as a Service (IaaS), Platform as a Service (PaaS), and Software as a Service (SaaS). These models offer varying levels of abstraction and control over computing resources, allowing users to access and utilize infrastructure, platforms, or software applications on-demand via the internet.

Overall, understanding and leveraging different system models in distributed and cloud computing environments is essential for designing scalable, resilient, and efficient systems to meet diverse computational needs and demands.

NIST Cloud Computing Reference Architecture

The NIST Cloud Computing Reference Architecture serves as a foundational framework for understanding and implementing cloud computing environments. Developed by the National Institute of Standards and Technology (NIST), this architecture provides a standardized approach to organizing and conceptualizing cloud systems, enabling interoperability, portability, and scalability across diverse cloud implementations.

At its core, the NIST Cloud Computing Reference Architecture defines various components and their relationships within a cloud environment. These components include:

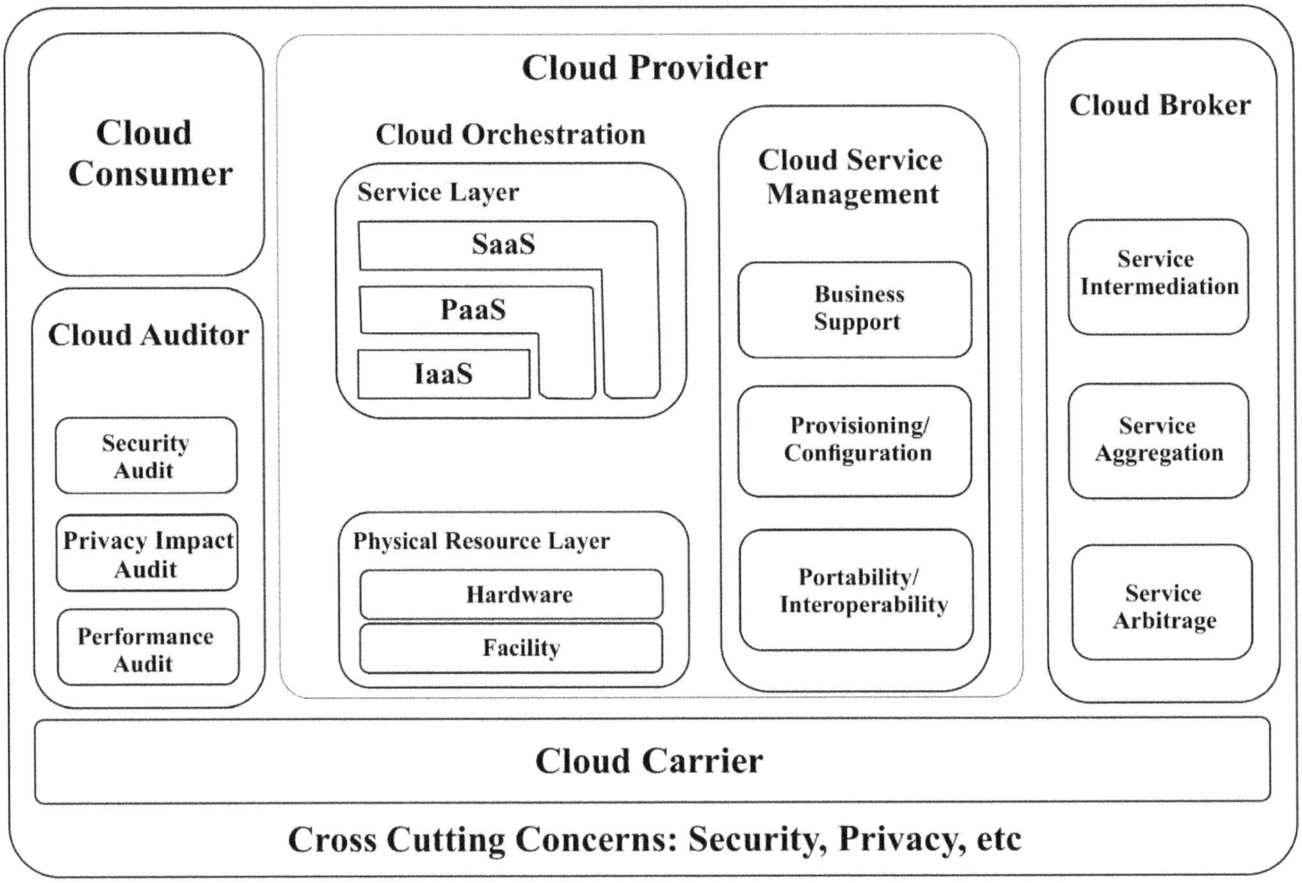

Cloud Service Consumer: Represents entities that consume cloud services, such as users, applications, or other systems.

Cloud Service Provider: Offers cloud services to consumers. This provider can be a public, private, community, or hybrid cloud provider.

Cloud Auditor: Ensures compliance, security, and governance within the cloud environment by auditing cloud services and operations.

Cloud Broker: Acts as an intermediary between cloud service providers and consumers, facilitating the selection, negotiation, and management of cloud services.

Cloud Carrier: Provides network connectivity and transport services for cloud consumers and providers.

Cloud Service: Represents the various services offered by cloud providers, such as Infrastructure as a Service (IaaS), Platform as a Service (PaaS), and Software as a Service (SaaS).

Cloud Service Management: Encompasses the processes and tools used to manage and administer cloud services, including provisioning, monitoring, and billing.

Cloud Resource Abstraction and Control: Refers to the mechanisms for abstracting and controlling underlying cloud resources, such as virtualization, orchestration, and automation.

Cloud Infrastructure: Includes the physical and virtual resources (e.g., servers, storage, networks) that constitute the cloud environment.

Cloud Federation: Involves the integration and interoperability of multiple cloud environments to provide seamless access to resources and services across clouds.

Cloud Security: Addresses the security measures and controls implemented to protect data, applications, and infrastructure in the cloud.

By delineating these components and their interactions, the NIST Cloud Computing Reference Architecture serves as a comprehensive guide for designing, deploying, and managing cloud environments that align with industry best practices and standards. It provides a common language and framework for stakeholders to communicate effectively and collaborate in the adoption and utilization of cloud computing technologies.

Cloud Deployment Models (Public, Private, Community, Hybrid)

Cloud deployment models categorize how cloud computing resources are provisioned and managed based on who can access them and how they are shared. The four primary cloud deployment models, as defined by the National Institute of Standards and Technology (NIST), are Public, Private, Community, and Hybrid.

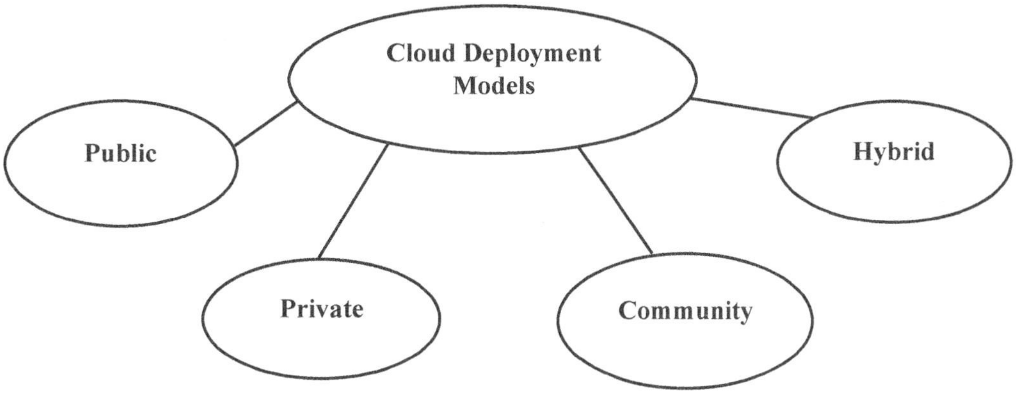

Here's an overview of each:

Public Cloud: In a public cloud deployment model, cloud services and resources are owned and operated by third-party providers, such as Amazon Web Services (AWS), Microsoft Azure, or Google Cloud Platform. These services are accessible to the general public over the internet on a pay-per-use basis. Public clouds offer scalability, cost-effectiveness, and convenience, making them suitable for a wide range of applications, from web hosting to big data analytics.

Private Cloud: A private cloud deployment model involves cloud services and resources that are dedicated solely to a single organization. These resources can be hosted either on-premises or externally by a third-party provider, but they are accessed exclusively by the organization and its authorized users. Private clouds offer greater control, customization, and security compared to public clouds, making them ideal for organizations with strict compliance requirements or sensitive data.

Community Cloud: Community cloud deployment models involve shared cloud resources that are accessed and utilized by a specific community of organizations or users with common concerns, such as regulatory compliance or industry-specific requirements. These resources may be managed by the community members themselves or by a third-party provider. Community clouds allow for collaboration, resource sharing, and cost-sharing among community members while providing more control and privacy compared to public clouds.

Hybrid Cloud: Hybrid cloud deployment models combine elements of public, private, and/or community clouds to create a unified, integrated infrastructure. Organizations leverage hybrid clouds to orchestrate workloads across multiple cloud environments, allowing them to optimize performance, cost, and scalability based on specific requirements and workload characteristics. Hybrid clouds offer flexibility, allowing organizations to maintain sensitive data and critical applications on-premises while leveraging the scalability and cost-effectiveness of public cloud services for other workloads.

Each cloud deployment model offers distinct advantages and considerations, and organizations often adopt a mix of these models based on their unique needs, regulatory requirements, and strategic objectives. Understanding the characteristics and trade-offs of each deployment model is essential for designing and implementing a cloud strategy that aligns with organizational goals.

Cloud Service Models (IaaS, PaaS, SaaS)

Cloud service models categorize the types of services and resources offered by cloud providers based on the level of abstraction and management provided to users. The three primary cloud service models, often referred to as the SPI model (Software, Platform, Infrastructure), are Infrastructure as a Service (IaaS), Platform as a Service (PaaS), and Software as a Service (SaaS).

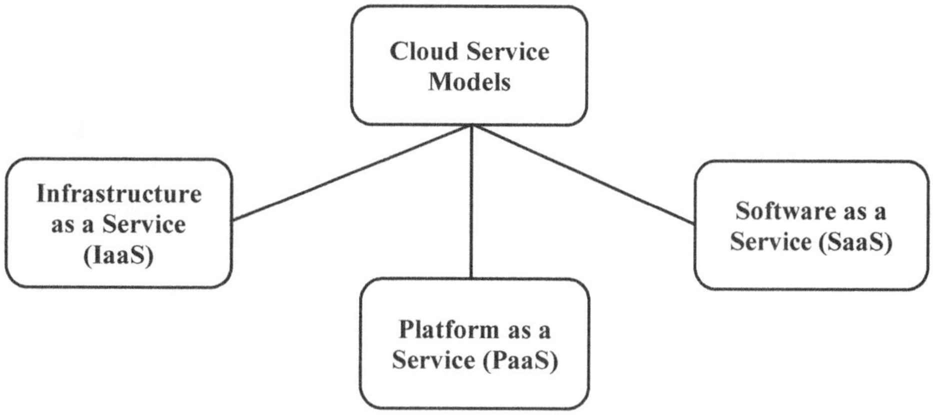

Here's a breakdown of each:

Infrastructure as a Service (IaaS):

In the IaaS model, cloud providers offer virtualized computing resources over the internet, including virtual machines, storage, and networking capabilities. Users have full control over the operating systems, applications, and development frameworks deployed on these virtualized resources.

IaaS enables organizations to provision and manage scalable infrastructure without the need to invest in and maintain physical hardware. Users can dynamically scale resources up or down based on demand, paying only for the resources they consume on a pay-per-use basis.

Examples of IaaS providers include Amazon Web Services (AWS) EC2, Microsoft Azure Virtual Machines, and Google Compute Engine.

Platform as a Service (PaaS):

PaaS provides a platform and environment for developing, deploying, and managing applications without the complexity of infrastructure management. Cloud providers offer a suite of development tools, middleware, and runtime environments that streamline the application development and deployment process.

PaaS abstracts away the underlying infrastructure, allowing developers to focus solely on building and deploying applications. It provides built-in scalability, security, and management features, enabling rapid development and deployment cycles.
Examples of PaaS offerings include AWS Elastic Beanstalk, Microsoft Azure App Service, and Google App Engine.

Software as a Service (SaaS):
SaaS delivers fully functional software applications over the internet on a subscription basis. Users access these applications through web browsers or APIs, without the need for installation or maintenance of software on local devices.
SaaS providers host and manage the entire software stack, including infrastructure, middleware, and application code. Users benefit from automatic updates, scalability, and accessibility from any device with an internet connection.
Examples of SaaS applications include Salesforce CRM, Google Workspace (formerly G Suite), and Microsoft Office 365.
Each cloud service model offers varying levels of abstraction and management, catering to different user needs and preferences. Organizations can choose the most suitable service model based on factors such as application requirements, development expertise, and operational considerations.

Summery

Client-Server Architecture: Centralized management and processing of data; clients request resources from centralized servers.
Peer-to-Peer (P2P) Architecture: Nodes act as both clients and servers, promoting decentralized resource sharing and scalability.
Service-Oriented Architecture (SOA): Organizes software components into network-accessible services, emphasizing modularity and interoperability.
Cloud Computing Models: IaaS provides virtualized resources, PaaS offers development platforms, and SaaS delivers fully functional applications over the internet.
Public Cloud: Owned by third-party providers, accessible to the general public, offering scalability and cost-effectiveness.
Private Cloud: Dedicated to a single organization, offering greater control, customization, and security.
Hybrid Cloud: Combines public, private, and/or community clouds, optimizing performance, cost, and scalability.
NIST Cloud Components: Includes Cloud Service Consumer, Cloud Service Provider, Cloud Auditor, Cloud Broker, Cloud Carrier, Cloud Service Management, and Cloud Security.

Glossary

Client-Server Architecture:A system model where clients request services from centralized servers, allowing centralized management and maintenance of data and applications.

Peer-to-Peer (P2P) Architecture:A decentralized system where nodes act as both clients and servers, promoting resource sharing and scalability without centralized infrastructure.

Service-Oriented Architecture (SOA): Organizes software components into network-accessible services, emphasizing modularity, interoperability, and reusability.

Infrastructure as a Service (IaaS): Provides virtualized computing resources over the internet, allowing users full control over the operating systems, applications, and frameworks.

Platform as a Service (PaaS): Offers a platform for developing, deploying, and managing applications, abstracting infrastructure management, and providing development tools and runtime environments.

Software as a Service (SaaS): Delivers fully functional software applications over the internet, managed by the provider, and accessed via web browsers or APIs.

Public Cloud: Services owned and operated by third-party providers, accessible to the general public on a pay-per-use basis, offering scalability and cost-effectiveness.

Private Cloud: Dedicated cloud resources for a single organization, offering greater control, customization, and security, either hosted on-premises or by a third-party provider.

Exercise

Exercise 1 – MCQ

1. Which system model in distributed computing involves a central server that manages clients and resources?

a. Client-Server

b. Peer-to-Peer

c. Distributed Ledger

d. Centralized Network

2. What does the NIST Cloud Computing Reference Architecture identify as a key actor responsible for providing cloud services to consumers?

a. Cloud Auditor

b. Cloud Broker

c. Cloud Provider

d. Cloud Carrier

Exercise 2 – True/ False

1. PaaS (Platform as a Service) includes hardware and software tools available over the internet but does not include development tools.

2. Community cloud models are used by organizations that have shared concerns and objectives, and the cloud infrastructure is shared among several organizations.

Exercise 3 – Fill in the blanks

1. The ____________ cloud deployment model is designed for exclusive use by a single organization, ensuring higher control and security.
2. In the NIST Cloud Computing Reference Architecture, the role responsible for managing the cloud infrastructure and ensuring that the cloud services are delivered as per the SLA is the ____________.

Exercise 4 – One-Word

1. Which system model is specifically designed to handle distributed applications by decentralizing resources and operations?
2. What type of cloud model involves sharing infrastructure between several organizations from a specific community with common concerns?

Exercise 5 – Small answer

1. What are the key differences between the public and private cloud deployment models?
2. Briefly describe the role of a cloud service provider in the NIST Cloud Computing Reference Architecture.

Exercise 6 – Long answer

1. Explain the NIST Cloud Computing Reference Architecture and discuss the roles and responsibilities defined within it.
2. Compare and contrast the different cloud service models (IaaS, PaaS, SaaS), highlighting their key features, advantages, and use cases.

Answer

Exercise 1 – MCQ

Ans: 1 a, 2 c.

Exercise 2 – True/False

Ans: 1 False, 2 True.

Exercise 3 – Fill in The Blanks

Ans: 1Private, 2 Cloud Provider.

Exercise 4 – One-Word

Ans: 1 Peer-to-Peer, 2 Community.

Online Resources

1. **True/False Practice Paper:** https://forms.gle/tpMDMAJ2s3EZMr8s6

QR Code:

2. **True/False Video Link:**
https://www.youtube.com/playlist?list=PLzlh_31VWEFpJXXMLkdAjocskNzX4YZZj

QR Code:

3. **One Word Practice Paper:** https://forms.gle/Ccdi84dLpoEcGpqj9

QR Code:

4. **One Word Video Link:**
https://www.youtube.com/playlist?list=PLzlh_31VWEFqnbfJX75VZPTneWnuduLIP

QR Code:

Chapter 3: Basics of Virtualization

Definition and Types of Virtualization

Virtualization is the process of creating a virtual version of something, such as hardware platforms, storage devices, network resources, or an operating system, where the framework divides the resource into one or more execution environments. Essentially, virtualization makes it possible to run multiple operating systems and applications on the same server simultaneously, maximizing the utilization of computing resources.

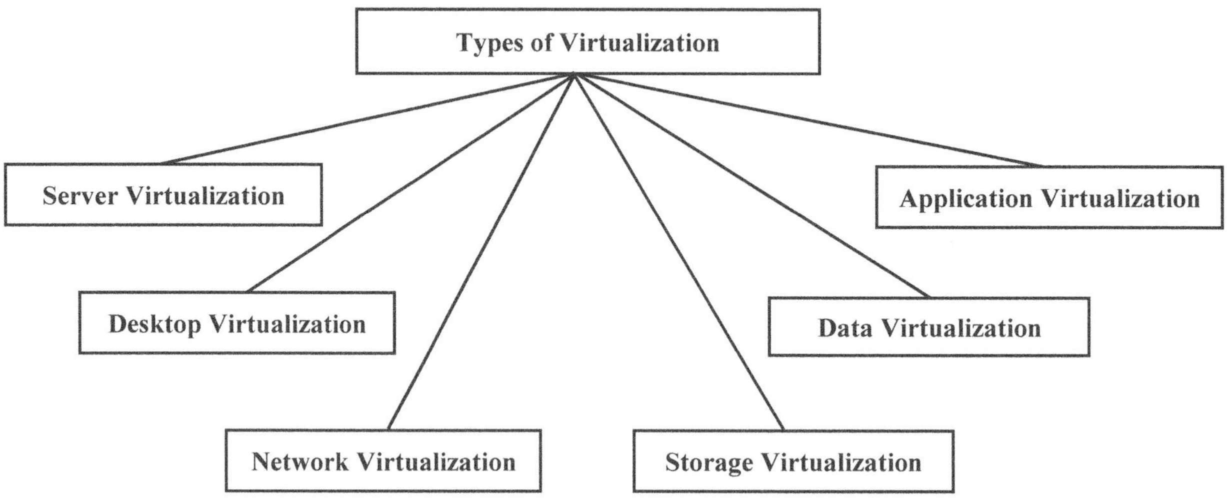

Types of Virtualization

Server Virtualization

This involves partitioning a physical server into smaller virtual servers. Each virtual server acts like a unique physical device, capable of running its own operating system independently. This type is widely used in data centres to optimize server resources and reduce hardware costs.

Desktop Virtualization

This type allows users to have their desktop hosted on a remote central server, enabling access to the desktop sessions over a network using a client device. This setup supports a flexible and secure workspace environment, as the desktop is maintained and controlled centrally.

Network Virtualization

Network virtualization combines hardware and software network resources and network functionality into a single, software-based administrative entity, a virtual network. This type helps in improving speed, scalability, and security within a network by managing the entire network as a single entity.

Storage Virtualization

This involves pooling physical storage from multiple network storage devices into what appears to be a single storage device that is managed from a central console. This type is beneficial for backup, archiving, and recovery processes, improving performance and scalability.

Data Virtualization

This technology abstracts the traditional technical details of data management, such as location, performance, or format, and allows high-level access via a single "virtual" data layer. Data virtualization tools and services provide real-time data integration without requiring physical consolidation.

Application Virtualization

This isolates applications from the underlying operating system on which they are executed. A virtualized application is not installed in the traditional sense, although it behaves as if it is. This can be used to resolve application conflicts and streamline application deployment.

Each type of virtualization has its own specific applications and can be chosen based on the needs of the business or technology environment, helping to drive efficiency, flexibility, and scalability in IT operations.

Taxonomy of Virtual Machines

Virtual machines (VMs) are an integral part of virtualization technology. They provide an environment that is logically isolated from the underlying hardware. VMs can run their own operating systems and applications as if they were separate physical entities. The taxonomy of virtual machines can be categorized based on their architecture and the level of abstraction they provide.

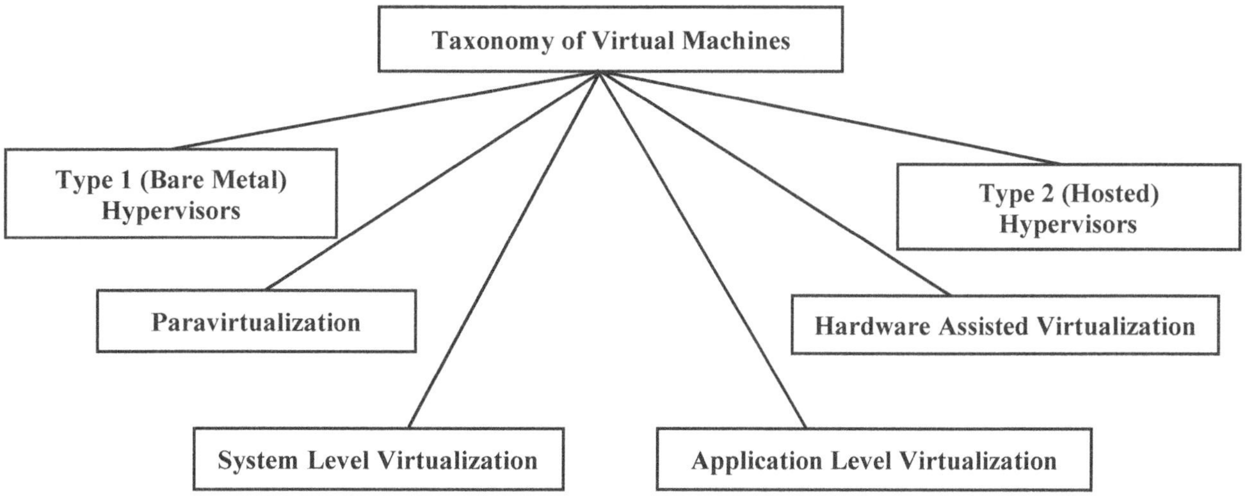

Here's a detailed breakdown:

Type 1 (Bare Metal) Hypervisors

These hypervisors run directly on the host's hardware to control the hardware and to manage guest operating systems. For this reason, they are considered more efficient as they have direct access to hardware resources. Examples include VMware ESXi, Microsoft Hyper-V, and Xen.

Type 2 (Hosted) Hypervisors

These hypervisors run on a conventional operating system just as other computer programs do. The hypervisor layer is a distinct second software level above the hardware and below the guest operating systems. Examples include VMware Workstation, Oracle VirtualBox, and Parallels Desktop.

Paravirtualization

Unlike full virtualization, where the hardware is completely simulated, paravirtualization involves the guest operating systems being aware of one another. This type of VM architecture can improve performance by reducing the hypervisor overhead since the guest OS is explicitly communicating with the host. An example is Xen in Para virtualized mode.

Hardware Assisted Virtualization

This uses processor-specific virtualization extensions that are built into the host's hardware, which help to execute what were traditionally non-virtualizable instructions. Examples of hardware-assisted virtualization include Intel VT and AMD-V.

System Level Virtualization

This provides a comprehensive platform that mimics the hardware and includes software execution layer interfaces. It offers an environment that allows all sub-systems to operate in an isolated and encapsulated manner. Linux Containers (LXC) and Docker are examples of system-level virtualization, where the kernel allows for multiple isolated user-space instances.

Application Level Virtualization

This focuses on running applications in environments that are abstracted from the underlying hardware they are executed on. This form of virtualization is handled at the application layer and can include applications running in isolated sandboxes that do not interfere with the global state of the system. Examples include Portable Apps and Cameo.

Each category of VMs offers distinct advantages and is suitable for different types of tasks. For instance, bare-metal hypervisors are ideal for environments requiring high performance and scalability, while hosted hypervisors are more suited for testing and development environments where flexibility and simplicity are more critical.

Hypervisor and Key Concepts

A hypervisor, also known as a virtual machine monitor (VMM), is a software, firmware, or hardware that creates and manages virtual machines (VMs). It allows multiple operating systems to run concurrently on a host machine by abstracting the guest operating systems from the host hardware. Hypervisors provide the foundation for virtualization and are critical for managing the system's resources among the various VMs.

Types of Hypervisors

Type 1 (Bare Metal) Hypervisors:

These hypervisors run directly on the system hardware, serving as the primary interface between the physical resources and the virtual environments. They offer better performance, scalability, and security, making them ideal for enterprise data centres. Examples include VMware ESXi, Microsoft Hyper-V, and Xen.

Type 2 (Hosted) Hypervisors:

These are installed on top of an existing operating system, and they rely on the host OS to manage and execute hardware calls. They are easier to install and manage but may offer reduced performance compared to Type 1 hypervisors. Common examples are VMware Workstation and Oracle VirtualBox.

Key Concepts in Hypervisor Technology

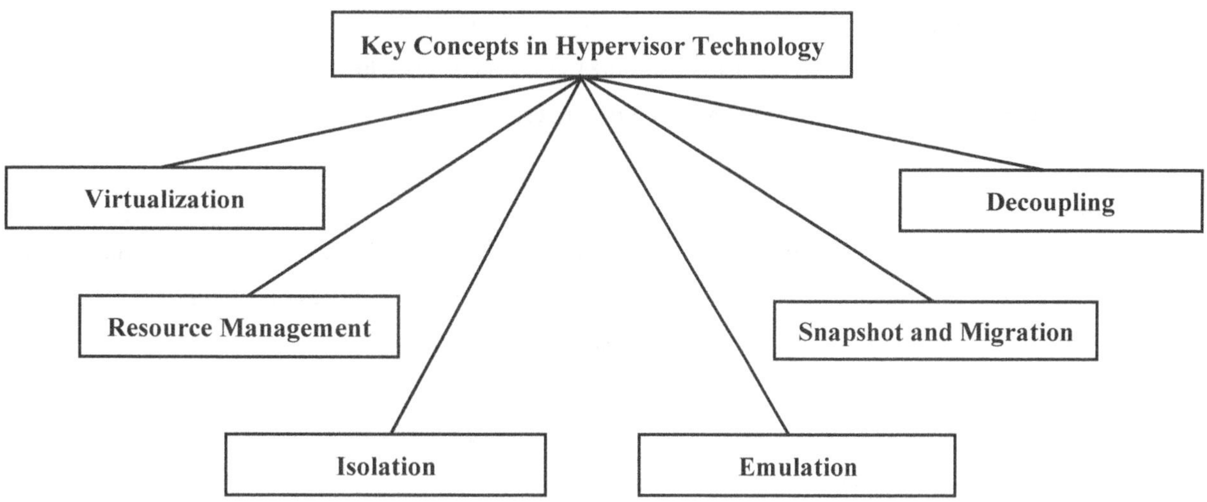

Virtualization:

The process of creating a virtual (rather than actual) version of something, including virtual computer hardware platforms, storage devices, and computer network resources.

Resource Management:

Hypervisors are responsible for distributing hardware resources such as CPU time, memory, bandwidth, and storage to each VM according to predefined configurations or dynamic resource scheduling algorithms.

Isolation:

Each virtual machine is isolated from others, ensuring that processes running in one VM do not interfere with those in another. This isolation helps improve security and system stability.

Emulation:

The hypervisor can emulate hardware functionalities for virtual machines, which may not have direct access to the underlying hardware. This is particularly important in Type 2 hypervisors, where the emulation can allow non-native applications to run on the host system.

Snapshot and Migration:

Hypervisors allow administrators to take snapshots of a virtual machine's state, which can be restored later. This is useful for backup and recovery. Live migration is another feature, allowing for the movement of a VM from one physical server to another without downtime, facilitating maintenance and load balancing.

Decoupling:

By decoupling the guest operating systems from the hardware, hypervisors enable a greater degree of flexibility in terms of the operating system configurations and applications that can be used on the hardware.

Understanding these concepts is essential for efficiently managing virtual environments and leveraging the full potential of virtualization technology. Hypervisors continue to play a crucial role in cloud computing, providing the groundwork for scalable, flexible, and secure computing resources.

Virtualization of CPU, Memory, and I/O Devices

Virtualization technology extends beyond just creating virtual machines; it also involves the virtualization of critical hardware resources like CPU, memory, and I/O devices. This process ensures that these resources can be efficiently shared among multiple virtual environments running on a single physical system.

CPU Virtualization

CPU virtualization involves the abstraction of the central processing unit resources to allow multiple operating systems to run concurrently on a single physical CPU. Hypervisors manage CPU virtualization by intercepting guest OS operations and translating them into operations on the host's physical CPU.

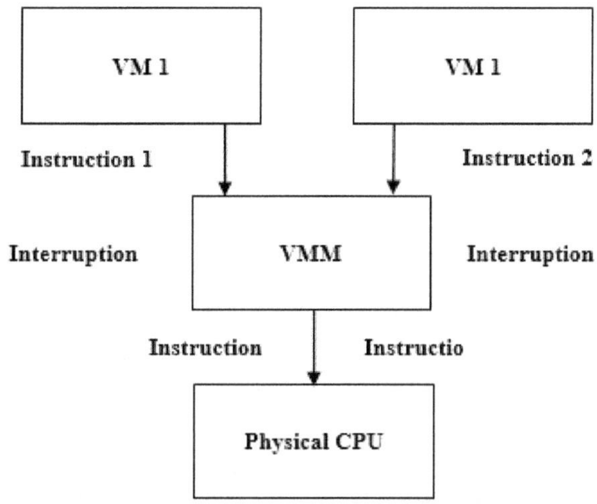

There are two primary methods used in CPU virtualization:

Full Virtualization - Utilizes hardware-assisted virtualization capabilities (such as Intel VT-x and AMD-V) to fully emulate a hardware platform that guest operating systems can run on. This allows the guest OS to operate as if it were running on its own hardware.

Paravirtualization - Involves a hypervisor providing an API that requires modifications to the guest OS to interact with it. This method reduces the overhead associated with emulating hardware, improving performance but at the cost of flexibility since the guest OS needs to be specifically tailored for the hypervisor.

Memory Virtualization

Memory virtualization involves the pooling of physical memory from multiple sources to create a virtual memory system that is managed centrally by the hypervisor.

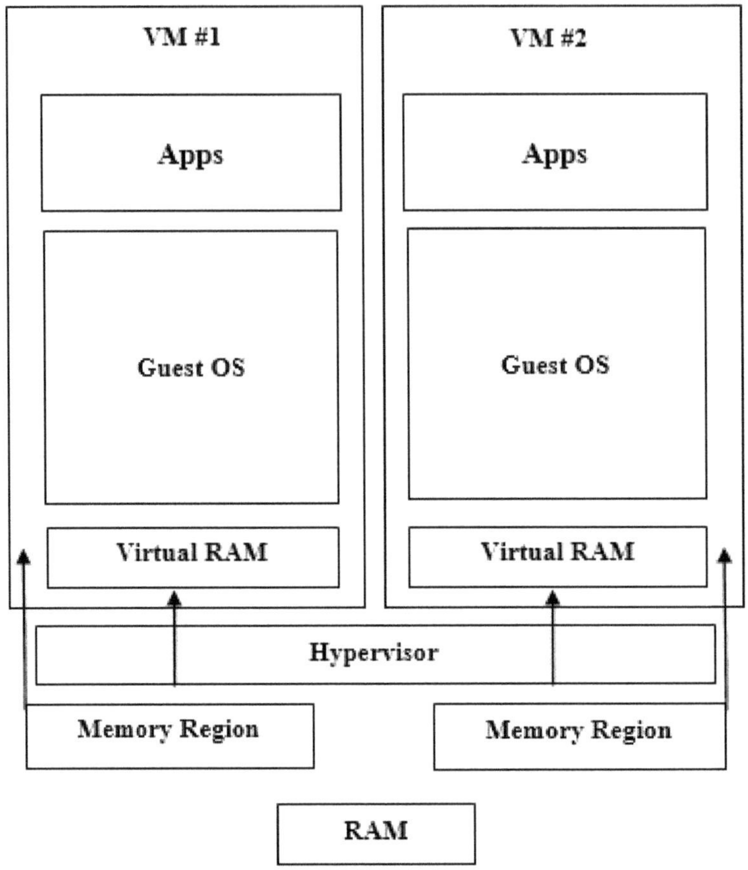

This allows for:

Transparent Page Sharing (TPS) - Identifies identical pages among different VMs and consolidates them into a single page, saving physical memory.

Balloon Drivers - Dynamically adjust the amount of physical memory available to each VM by inflating (using up) memory space temporarily when the host needs more physical memory resources.

Overcommitment - Allocates more memory to the virtual machines than the actual physical memory available, banking on the fact that not all VMs will use their allocated memory at the same time.

I/O Device Virtualization

I/O virtualization is the technique of abstracting and managing input/output operations from various hardware devices, such as network interfaces and storage devices, across multiple virtual machines.

This is accomplished through:

Direct I/O - Allows VMs to directly access physical hardware devices, reducing hypervisor overhead but increasing potential security risks.

I/O Virtualization (IOV) - Utilizes technologies like Single Root I/O Virtualization (SR-IOV) to bypass the hypervisor and provide VMs direct access to I/O devices, improving performance and reducing latency.

Virtual I/O (VIO) - Uses virtual devices that are managed by the hypervisor, which then translates these operations to real devices. This method offers greater flexibility and security at the expense of some performance.

Overall, virtualization of CPU, memory, and I/O devices is critical for optimizing resource utilization, improving performance, enhancing security, and ensuring operational flexibility in virtual environments. These technologies form the backbone of modern data centres and cloud computing platforms, enabling scalable and efficient management of large-scale computing resources.

Summary

Virtualization creates virtual versions of hardware platforms, storage devices, network resources, or operating systems, allowing multiple OSs and applications to run on the same server.

Server Virtualization partitions physical servers into virtual servers, optimizing resources and reducing costs.

Desktop Virtualization hosts user desktops on remote servers, enabling network access and centralized management.

Network Virtualization combines network resources into a single software-based entity, improving speed, scalability, and security.

Storage Virtualization pools physical storage into a single managed entity, enhancing backup, archiving, and recovery.

Hypervisors manage VMs, allowing multiple OSs to run concurrently on a host machine. Type 1 hypervisors run directly on hardware, providing better performance and security (e.g., VMware ESXi), while Type 2 hypervisors run on top of an existing OS (e.g., VMware Workstation).

CPU Virtualization includes full virtualization using hardware-assisted capabilities and paravirtualization with direct hypervisor interaction.

Memory Virtualization uses techniques like Transparent Page Sharing (TPS), balloon drivers, and overcommitment for efficient memory management.

Glossary

Virtualization: The process of creating virtual versions of hardware platforms, storage devices, network resources, or operating systems to maximize resource utilization.

Server Virtualization: Partitioning a physical server into smaller virtual servers, each capable of running its own operating system independently.

Desktop Virtualization: Hosting user desktops on a remote central server, enabling network access and centralized management of desktop sessions.

Network Virtualization: Combining hardware and software network resources into a single, software-based virtual network to improve speed, scalability, and security.

Storage Virtualization: Pooling physical storage from multiple devices into a single managed entity for enhanced backup, archiving, and recovery processes.

Data Virtualization: Abstracting traditional data management details, allowing high-level access via a virtual data layer without physical consolidation.

Application Virtualization: Isolating applications from the underlying operating system, allowing them to run as if they were installed traditionally, resolving conflicts, and streamlining deployment.

Type 1 (Bare Metal) Hypervisors: Hypervisors that run directly on the host's hardware, providing efficient control of resources (e.g., VMware ESXi, Microsoft Hyper-V).

Type 2 (Hosted) Hypervisors: Hypervisors that run on an existing operating system, acting as a second layer above the hardware (e.g., VMware Workstation, Oracle VirtualBox).

Paravirtualization:A VM architecture where guest operating systems are aware of each other, reducing hypervisor overhead (e.g., Xen in Para virtualized mode).

Hardware Assisted Virtualization: Uses processor-specific extensions to execute traditionally non-virtualizable instructions (e.g., Intel VT, AMD-V).

System Level Virtualization: Mimics hardware and includes software execution layer interfaces, allowing multiple isolated user-space instances (e.g., Linux Containers, Docker).

Application Level Virtualization: Runs applications in environments abstracted from the underlying hardware, often in isolated sandboxes (e.g., Portable Apps, Cameo).

Hypervisor (VMM): Software, firmware, or hardware that creates and manages virtual machines, allowing multiple operating systems to run concurrently on a host machine.

CPU Virtualization: Abstraction of CPU resources to allow multiple operating systems to run concurrently on a single physical CPU.

Memory Virtualization: Pooling physical memory from multiple sources into a centrally managed virtual memory system.

I/O Virtualization: Abstracting and managing input/output operations from hardware devices across multiple virtual machines.

Exercise

Exercise 1 – MCQ

1. What type of virtual machine runs directly on the host's hardware without a host operating system?

a. Type 1 Hypervisor

b. Type 2 Hypervisor

c. VirtualBox

d. VMware Workstation

2. Which hypervisor type requires a host operating system to function?

a. Type 1 Hypervisor

b. Type 2 Hypervisor

c. Both Type 1 and Type 2

d. None of the above

Exercise 2 – True/ False

1. Virtualization of I/O devices is not possible; only CPU and memory can be virtualized.

2. One key concept of virtualization is the ability of a virtual machine to execute non-privileged code directly on the physical hardware for performance efficiency.

Exercise 3 – Fill in the blanks

1. A ____________ is a software layer that allows multiple virtual machines to run on a single physical host by managing the hardware resources.

2. ____________ virtualization allows multiple operating systems to share the same hardware resources by abstracting the underlying physical hardware.

Exercise 4 – One-Word

1. Which type of virtual machine runs directly on the hardware without a host OS?

2. What is the software layer that enables virtualization by managing virtual machines?

Exercise 5 – Small answer

1. What is the primary function of a hypervisor in virtualization?

2. Briefly explain the difference between Type 1 and Type 2 hypervisors.

Exercise 6 – Long answer

1. Describe the different types of virtualization and provide examples of each type, highlighting their practical applications.

2. Explain the concept of virtualizing CPU, memory, and I/O devices in the context of virtualization. How does this enhance the efficiency of computing resources?

Answer

Exercise 1 – MCQ

Ans: 1 a, 2 b.

Exercise 2 – True/False

Ans: 1 False, 2 True.

Exercise 3 – Fill in The Blanks

Ans: 1Hypervisor, 2 Five

Exercise 4 – One-Word

Ans: 1.Type 1, 2.Hypervisor.

Online Resources

True/False Practice Paper : **https://forms.gle/Uax1evvDZxfvBAq89**

QR Code:

True/False Video Link :

https://www.youtube.com/playlist?list=PLzlh_31VWEFqlqXofU02o2EJN0TgWSqkR

QR Code:

One Word Practice Paper: **https://forms.gle/etom8oKin6t1VQzz5**

QR Code:

One Word Video Link: **https://www.youtube.com/playlist?list=PLzlh_31VWEFoVS2oLEx33VfLEa8p97YT4**

QR Code:

Chapter 4: Types of Cloud Services

Software as a Service (SaaS)

Software as a Service (SaaS) is a software distribution model in which applications are hosted by a third-party provider and made available to customers over the internet. This model allows users to access software applications on a subscription basis without the need for internal infrastructure or hardware.

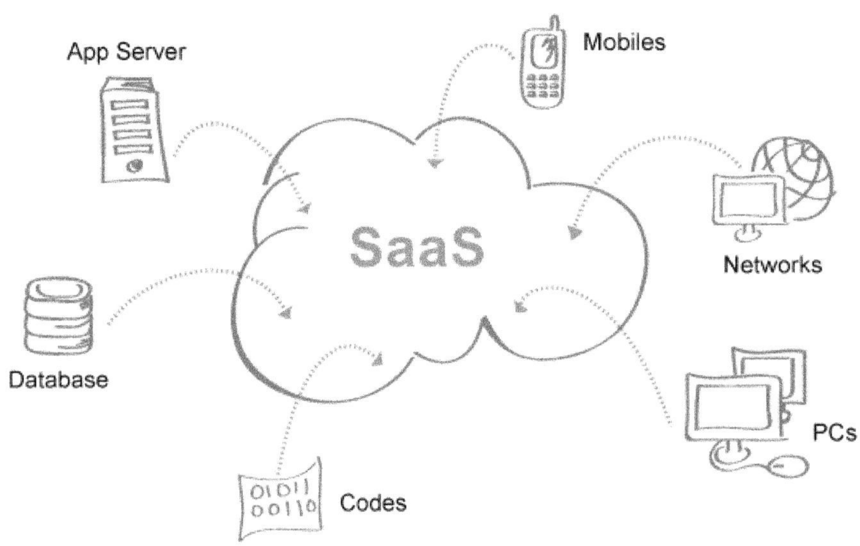

Key characteristics of SaaS include:

Accessibility: Users can access SaaS applications from any internet-enabled device, enhancing mobility and flexibility.

Scalability: SaaS providers typically offer various subscription levels, allowing businesses to scale services according to their needs without major upfront investments.

Maintenance: The SaaS provider handles all maintenance tasks, including updates and bug fixes, which reduces the workload for customer IT departments.

Advantages of SaaS

Cost-Effective: Reduces the cost of software ownership by eliminating the need for hardware acquisitions, full software licenses, maintenance fees, and installation and support services.

Quick Deployment: SaaS applications are already installed and configured in the cloud. This minimizes common delays resulting from lengthy traditional software deployment.

Automatic Updates: Users can rely on the SaaS provider to automatically perform updates and patch management, which helps secure the software and reduce the burden on internal IT staff.

Flexibility and Scalability: Users can subscribe to services with different feature sets and scalability options to meet fluctuating workload demands.

Common Use Cases

Customer Relationship Management (CRM): Tools like Salesforce allow businesses to manage and analyze customer interactions and data throughout the customer lifecycle.

Human Resources Management: Solutions such as Workday provide recruiting, training, payroll, and benefits management all in one platform.

Enterprise Resource Planning (ERP): Platforms like SAP and Oracle offer comprehensive business management tools covering everything from production to service delivery.

Collaboration and Productivity: Applications such as Google Workspace and Microsoft 365 enable teams to collaborate in real time on documents and projects.

Challenges and Considerations

Data Security: While SaaS providers generally offer robust security measures, relying on third-party services can pose risks related to data breaches and loss.

Compliance and Privacy: Organizations need to ensure that their SaaS providers comply with relevant regulations and standards, such as GDPR, HIPAA, or SOX.

Vendor Lock-in: Switching SaaS providers can be difficult and costly, as exporting and transferring large data sets to another platform often involves complexities and compatibility issues.

Platform as a Service (PaaS)

Platform as a Service (PaaS) is a cloud computing model that provides customers with a platform to develop, run, and manage applications without the complexity of building and maintaining the infrastructure typically associated with developing and launching an app. PaaS can be thought of as a layer on top of Infrastructure as a Service (IaaS) and below Software as a Service (SaaS) in the cloud service model hierarchy.

Key features include:

Development Tools: PaaS provides a suite of development tools that can include programming languages, libraries, a development environment, and pre-configured app components.

Middleware: Automatically handles the integration of databases, web servers, and business analytics into your applications.

Operating Systems: Users can develop on a framework without worrying about OS updates and patches.

Database Management: Includes management tools for handling large databases without the need for deep database administration expertise.

Scalability: Resources can scale automatically to match the application's needs without any manual intervention from developers.

Advantages of PaaS

Reduced Development Time: By offering software components that are ready to use, PaaS allows developers to cut down on coding time, enabling faster deployment.

Cost Efficiency: Reduces costs by eliminating the need to invest in physical hardware, software licenses, and other infrastructure expenses.

Multi-tenant Architecture: Allows multiple users to develop applications using a single development application.

Development Simplification: Provides all of the capabilities needed to support the complete web application lifecycle: building, testing, deploying, managing, and updating within the same integrated environment.

Common Use Cases

Web Application Development: Enables developers to concentrate on the development of their application without having to manage the underlying infrastructure.

API Development: Supports the creation, hosting, and management of APIs with tools to handle heavy traffic and security.

Real-Time Application Development: Ideal for applications that require real-time collaboration capabilities.

Internet of Things (IoT) Applications: Provides a robust and scalable environment to handle and process data from IoT devices.

Challenges and Considerations

Limited Control: While PaaS provides many conveniences, it also restricts the ability of developers to control underlying infrastructure, which can be problematic for applications requiring specific environment configurations.

Data Security: The shared nature of the platform can pose potential security risks, especially for applications that manage sensitive data.

Vendor Lock-in: PaaS solutions may lead to vendor lock-in, making it difficult to migrate to another platform due to the use of vendor-specific features and APIs.

Infrastructure as a Service (IaaS)

Infrastructure as a Service (IaaS) is a form of cloud computing that provides virtualized computing resources over the internet. IaaS is one of the three main categories of cloud services, alongside Software as a Service (SaaS) and Platform as a Service (PaaS). This model enables organizations to rent or lease servers for compute and storage in the cloud, where they can install operating systems, applications, and databases.

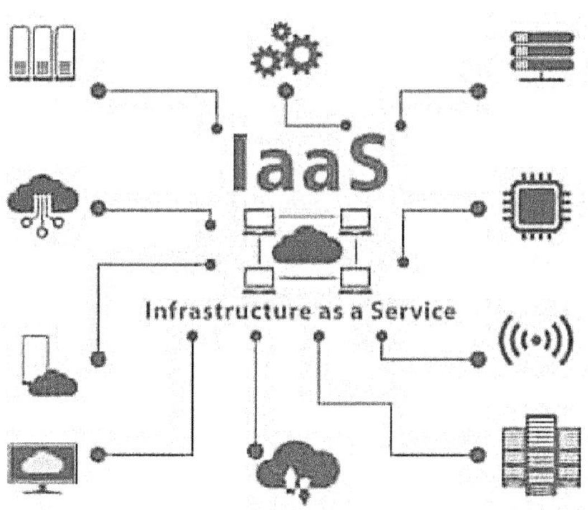

Characteristics of IaaS include:

Scalability: Resources can be scaled up or down quickly based on demand, which is ideal for businesses experiencing fluctuating workloads.

Flexibility: Users have control over their infrastructure, more so than with PaaS or SaaS offerings, including choices of operating systems, hardware, and network features.

Utility Costing: Clients pay only for the resources they use, which often leads to cost savings compared to managing physical servers.

Advantages of IaaS

Cost-Effective: Reduces the need for expensive hardware investments. Organizations can simply pay as they go and for what they use.

Business Continuity and Disaster Recovery: Enhances business continuity capabilities due to data being stored in the cloud, spreading infrastructure risk.

Focus on Core Business: Allows companies to focus more on their core business rather than infrastructure management.

Innovation: Provides the flexibility to experiment and innovate more easily by setting up and dismantling test environments without incurring significant infrastructure expenses.

Common Use Cases

Website Hosting: More flexible and scalable than traditional hosting at often lower costs.

Virtual Data Centers: Provides a complete virtual network including virtual machines, routers, bandwidth, and firewalls in a fully virtualized environment.

High-Performance Computing: Users can perform complex calculations on large datasets using IaaS.

Big Data Analysis: Offers powerful servers and optimal storage solutions necessary for mining massive amounts of data to identify patterns and insights.

Challenges and Considerations

Security Concerns: Although cloud providers implement robust security measures, hosting sensitive data and critical applications off-site can pose potential security risks.

Management Complexity: While IaaS offers more control, it also requires IT expertise to manage the infrastructure, which may be a challenge for smaller businesses without dedicated IT teams.

Network Dependence: Since the infrastructure is accessed over the Internet, a stable and fast internet connection is critical for accessing services without interruption.

Database as a Service (DBaaS)

Database as a Service (DBaaS) is a cloud computing service that provides users with access to a database without requiring the setup, configuration, and management of the physical database infrastructure. DBaaS is a category of cloud services that allows developers, analysts, and IT professionals to leverage the database functionality without the complexity and overhead of hardware provisioning and software maintenance.

Key features include:

Automated Management: DBaaS providers handle routine tasks such as provisioning, backups, updates, and scaling.

Accessibility: Databases are accessible from anywhere, making it easier for distributed teams to collaborate and for applications to interact with the database from any location.

Scalability: Resources can be scaled up or down automatically or on demand, depending on the workload, which is ideal for variable performance needs.

Multi-Tenancy: Multiple users can manage and operate their databases independently within a shared infrastructure, optimizing resource utilization.

Advantages of DBaaS

Cost Efficiency: Reduces the need to purchase hardware or hire specialized staff to manage database operations, significantly lowering the cost of database management.

Focus on Innovation: Frees up IT staff from routine database maintenance tasks, allowing them to focus on more strategic activities that add business value.

Enhanced Scalability: Enables businesses to handle increasing data loads without the need to manually add hardware or reconfigure databases.

Improved Security: Often includes built-in security features such as data encryption, access controls, and regular security audits to protect sensitive data.

Common Use Cases

Web and Mobile Applications: Ideal for backing web and mobile applications where scalability and accessibility are critical.

Big Data Analytics: Provides the infrastructure necessary to perform real-time analytics on large datasets.

Development and Testing: Offers developers and testers a real-time, scalable environment to develop, test, and iterate on applications.

Disaster Recovery: Ensures data redundancy and enhances data integrity, providing backup mechanisms and data recovery in case of a disaster.

Challenges and Considerations

Data Security: While DBaaS providers generally offer strong security measures, the responsibility of securing access to and use of the database still largely falls on the customer.

Vendor Lock-in: Customers may become dependent on a particular DBaaS provider's tools and services, making it difficult to migrate to another provider without significant costs and complexities.

Performance Variability: Since databases are hosted in shared environments, "noisy neighbours" can potentially impact performance, although premium service levels can mitigate this.

Monitoring as a Service (MaaS)

Monitoring as a Service (MaaS) is a cloud-based approach that provides remote monitoring of IT infrastructure, applications, and services. It is designed to help organizations manage their networks, systems, and applications effectively by offering real-time visibility and reporting capabilities.

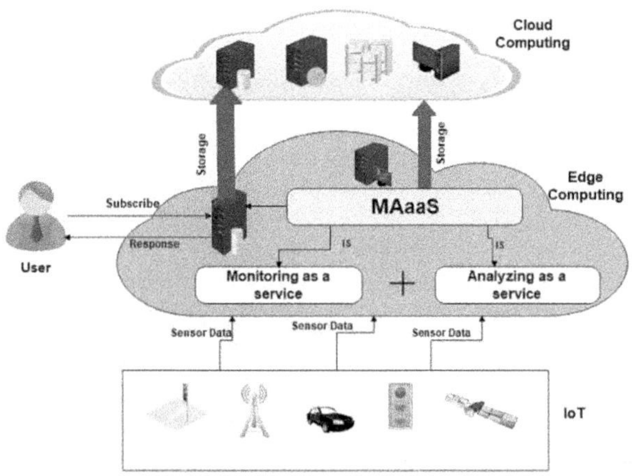

Key features of MaaS include:

Real-Time Monitoring: Continuously tracks the health and performance of IT assets and systems, providing alerts on issues as they arise.

Scalability: Can easily scale up or down based on the size and complexity of the monitored environments.

Centralized Management: Offers a single pane of glass for viewing all monitoring data, making it easier to oversee large and distributed environments.

Automated Alerts: Automatically sends notifications to IT staff via emails, SMS, or other communication tools when potential issues are detected.

Advantages of MaaS

Cost Reduction: Eliminates the need for significant upfront investment in monitoring infrastructure and reduces ongoing operational costs.

Enhanced Operational Efficiency: Automates many monitoring tasks, freeing up IT personnel to focus on more strategic initiatives.

Improved Uptime: Helps ensure higher levels of system availability by enabling proactive management and quick resolution of issues.

Flexibility: Offers flexible deployment options and can be integrated with existing IT management tools and processes.

Common Use Cases

Network Monitoring: Tracks the performance and availability of network components such as routers, switches, and firewalls.

Application Performance Monitoring (APM): Provides insights into application behaviour to optimize performance and improve user experience.

Server Monitoring: Oversees server health, utilization, and performance to prevent downtime and maintain operational continuity.

Security Monitoring: Continuously monitors for security threats and vulnerabilities, helping to ensure compliance with data protection regulations.

Challenges and Considerations

Data Privacy and Security: As with any cloud service, there is the challenge of ensuring that sensitive monitoring data is securely handled and stored.

Integration Complexity: Integrating MaaS solutions with existing IT infrastructure and workflows can be complex, particularly in hybrid or multi-cloud environments.

Dependency on Service Providers: Relying on third-party providers for critical monitoring tasks can pose risks, especially if the provider experiences downtime or service interruptions.

Communication as a Service (CaaS)

Communication as a Service (CaaS) is a cloud-based delivery model that allows businesses to outsource their communication needs, such as voice, video, and messaging services, to a third-party provider. It is designed to streamline communication processes by integrating various communication tools into a single, unified solution that can be managed remotely.

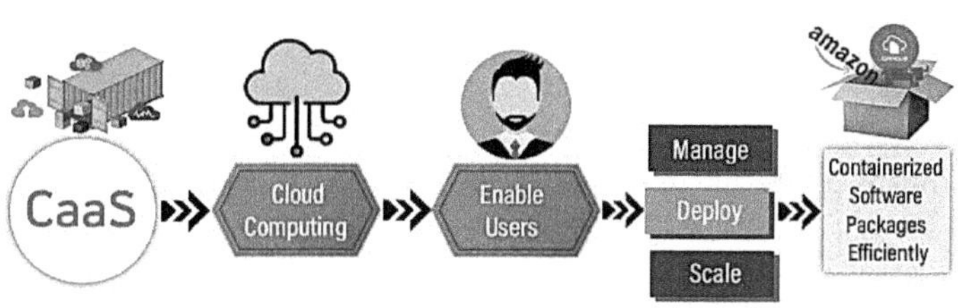

Key features of CaaS include:

Unified Communications: Integrates voice, video, chat, and email services into a unified platform that enhances collaboration.

Scalability: Enables businesses to scale communication capabilities up or down based on their needs without significant capital investment.

Mobility: Allows users to access communication tools from any device, anywhere, enhancing flexibility and connectivity.

Maintenance and Upgrades: The service provider manages all maintenance, upgrades, and support, ensuring that the communication systems are always up-to-date with the latest technologies.

Advantages of CaaS

Cost Efficiency: Reduces the need for in-house communication infrastructure and lowers overall IT costs by shifting to a subscription-based model.

Enhanced Collaboration: Facilitates better team collaboration through advanced communication tools that support real-time sharing and collaboration across different locations.

Reliability: Typically offers high availability and redundancy, ensuring reliable communication services that are crucial for business operations.

Regulatory Compliance: Ensures that communication services comply with relevant regulations, such as GDPR for data protection, without requiring businesses to manage compliance on their own.

Common Use Cases

Remote Work: Supports a distributed workforce with reliable tools for voice and video conferencing, instant messaging, and file sharing.

Customer Support Centres: Empowers support centres with advanced call routing, multi-channel support, and integrated customer relationship management (CRM) systems.

Event Broadcasting: Facilitates large-scale webinars and virtual events with tools for video broadcasting, attendee management, and interactive features.

Enterprise Communications: Integrates with enterprise systems to provide seamless communication capabilities across large organizations.

Challenges and Considerations

Service Quality: Dependence on the internet connection means that service quality can be impacted by bandwidth and network reliability.

Security Risks: Hosting communication data off-site raises concerns about data security and privacy, necessitating strong security measures from the provider.

Vendor Lock-in: Custom solutions and integrations may lead to dependency on a single provider, making it challenging to switch services without significant costs or disruptions.

Summary

Software as a Service (SaaS) provides applications hosted by a third-party, accessible via the internet, with scalable subscription levels and maintenance handled by the provider.

SaaS offers cost-effective solutions, quick deployment, automatic updates, and flexible, scalable services.

Common use cases for SaaS include CRM, human resources management, ERP, and collaboration tools.

Challenges with SaaS include data security risks, compliance issues, and potential vendor lock-in.

Platform as a Service (PaaS) offers a platform for developing, running, and managing applications with integrated development tools, middleware, and scalability.

PaaS reduces development time, costs, and simplifies the development process, making it ideal for web application and API development.

Challenges with PaaS include limited control over infrastructure, data security concerns, and vendor lock-in.

Infrastructure as a Service (IaaS) provides virtualized computing resources, offering scalability, flexibility, and utility costing.

IaaS is cost-effective, supports business continuity, and allows a focus on core business functions, with use cases like website hosting and big data analysis.

Challenges with IaaS include security concerns, management complexity, and dependence on network reliability.

Database as a Service (DBaaS) offers access to databases without managing physical infrastructure, with automated management, scalability, and accessibility.

DBaaS is cost-efficient, enhances innovation, and provides improved security, suitable for web and mobile applications, and big data analytics.

Challenges with DBaaS include data security responsibility, vendor lock-in, and potential performance variability.

Glossary

SaaS (Software as a Service): A software distribution model where applications are hosted by a third-party provider and accessed over the internet, allowing users to use software on a subscription basis without internal infrastructure.

Accessibility (SaaS): Ability to access SaaS applications from any internet-enabled device, enhancing mobility and flexibility.

Scalability (SaaS): Capability to scale services according to needs without major upfront investments.

Maintenance (SaaS): SaaS providers handle all maintenance tasks, including updates and bug fixes.

CRM (Customer Relationship Management): Tools like Salesforce that help businesses manage and analyze customer interactions and data.

PaaS (Platform as a Service): A cloud computing model providing a platform to develop, run, and manage applications without maintaining the infrastructure.

Development Tools (PaaS): Suite of tools including programming languages, libraries, and pre-configured app components.

Middleware (PaaS): Integration of databases, web servers, and business analytics into applications automatically.

IaaS (Infrastructure as a Service): Cloud service providing virtualized computing resources over the internet, allowing organizations to rent servers for compute and storage.

Scalability (IaaS): Ability to scale resources quickly based on demand.

Flexibility (IaaS): Users have control over their infrastructure, including choices of operating systems, hardware, and network features.

DBaaS (Database as a Service): Cloud computing service providing access to a database without managing physical infrastructure, with automated management, scalability, and accessibility.

Automated Management (DBaaS): DBaaS providers handle routine tasks like provisioning, backups, updates, and scaling.

MaaS (Monitoring as a Service): Cloud-based approach for remote monitoring of IT infrastructure, applications, and services, providing real-time visibility and reporting.

Real-Time Monitoring (MaaS): Continuous tracking of the health and performance of IT assets and systems.

CaaS (Communication as a Service): Cloud-based delivery model outsourcing communication needs like voice, video, and messaging services to a third-party provider.

Unified Communications (CaaS): Integration of voice, video, chat, and email services into a single platform.

Exercise

Exercise 1 – MCQ

1. What does Infrastructure as a Service (IaaS) typically provide to customers?

a. Data management software

b. Virtual machines and storage

c. Web-based applications

d. Communication tools

2. What is Database as a Service (DBaaS) primarily focused on providing?

a. Software tools for database creation and maintenance

b. Physical database servers and storage

c. Managed database platforms that are fully maintained by the provider

d. Direct access to raw database files

Exercise 2 – True/ False

1. Monitoring as a Service (MaaS) is primarily used for security monitoring and does not concern performance metrics.

2. Communication as a Service (CaaS) is a cloud service model that allows businesses to outsource their communication platforms, like email only.

Exercise 3 – Fill in the blanks

1. ___________ provides a platform allowing customers to develop, run, and manage applications without dealing with the underlying infrastructure.

2. ___________ allows users to access, manage, and utilize database services over the cloud without handling the database software or hardware directly.

Exercise 4 – One-Word

1. Which cloud service type provides virtualized computing resources over the internet?

2. Which service is specifically designed to offer database management systems as a cloud service?

Exercise 5 – Small answer

1. What is the primary difference between Software as a Service (SaaS) and Infrastructure as a Service (IaaS)?

2. Explain the role of Monitoring as a Service (MaaS) in cloud computing.

Exercise 6 – Long answer

1. Compare and contrast the different types of cloud services: SaaS, PaaS, and IaaS. Provide examples of each and discuss their advantages and disadvantages.

2. Discuss the significance of Communication as a Service (CaaS) and how it integrates with other cloud services to enhance business operations.

Answer

Exercise 1 – MCQ

Ans: 1 b, 2 c.

Exercise 2 – True/False

Ans: 1 False, 2 False.

Exercise 3 – Fill in The Blanks

Ans: 1Platform as a Service (PaaS), 2 Database as a Service (DBaaS).

Exercise 4 – One-Word

Ans: 1 IaaS, 2 DBaaS.

Online Resources

1. True/False Practice Paper: https://forms.gle/rHN12UasjEXeed7A7

QR Code :

2.True/False Video Link:

https://www.youtube.com/playlist?list=PLzlh_31VWEFo2uB8sbu4RnZu8AH5rQGet

QR Code :

3. One Word Practice Paper: https://forms.gle/ntKHSZkN5fKnBSTH6

QR Code :

4.One Word Video Link:

https://www.youtube.com/playlist?list=PLzlh_31VWEFrqQZfeUs9MQ3x1RmKnW4fn

QR Code :

Chapter 5: Cloud Deployment Environment

Major cloud service providers: Google App Engine, Amazon AWS, Microsoft Azure

The cloud computing landscape is dominated by several major providers, each offering unique services tailored to various business needs. Among the most prominent are Google App Engine, Amazon AWS, and Microsoft Azure. These platforms provide a wide range of cloud services including Infrastructure as a Service (IaaS), Platform as a Service (PaaS), and Software as a Service (SaaS), addressing everything from basic web hosting to complex machine learning applications.

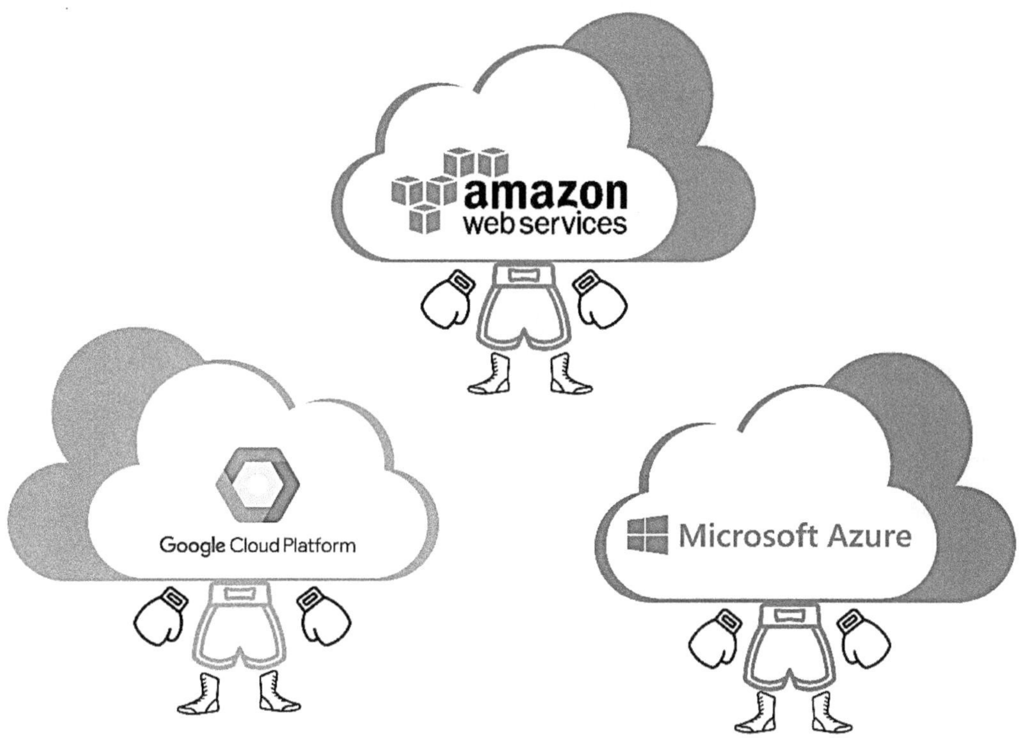

Google App Engine

Features and Strengths:

PaaS Offering: Google App Engine is a robust PaaS solution that lets developers build and deploy applications without managing the underlying infrastructure.

Scalability: Automatically scales depending on application demand and adjusts the resources needed, so developers don't need to worry about capacity planning.

Integrated Services: Offers tight integration with other Google services, such as Big Query, Google Kubernetes Engine, and TensorFlow, providing a comprehensive environment for developing, deploying, and enhancing applications.

Language Support: Supports multiple programming languages such as Python, Java, Ruby, C#, Go, Node.js, and PHP.

Amazon Web Services (AWS)

Features and Strengths:

Extensive Service Offering: AWS provides a vast array of services including EC2 for virtual servers, S3 for storage, and RDS for databases, making it suitable for virtually any cloud computing needs.

Market Leader: As a pioneer in the cloud industry, AWS offers unmatched experience, reliability, and a mature ecosystem.

Global Reach: Maintains an extensive global network of data centers, ensuring reduced latency and higher redundancy for international operations.

Innovative Technologies: Continuously introduces new technologies and tools in areas like AI, IoT, and quantum computing, helping users stay at the forefront of innovation.

Microsoft Azure

Features and Strengths:

Hybrid Capabilities: Strongly focuses on hybrid cloud solutions, making it easier for enterprises to integrate their on-premises infrastructure with the cloud.

Enterprise Integration: Offers seamless integration with Microsoft products such as Office 365, Active Directory, and SQL Server, which is a significant advantage for organizations already embedded in the Microsoft ecosystem.

Developer Tools: Provides powerful development tools like Azure DevOps, Visual Studio Code, and Azure Kubernetes Service (AKS) to support modern application development practices.

AI and Analytics: Features comprehensive tools for AI, machine learning, and analytics, including Azure Machine Learning, Azure Cognitive Services, and Azure Synapse Analytics.

Comparative Considerations

Choosing between these cloud service providers often depends on specific business requirements:

Existing Infrastructure: Enterprises heavily invested in Microsoft software might lean towards Azure for better integration.

Innovative Needs: Companies looking for the cutting-edge in cloud technology might prefer AWS due to its breadth of services and innovation.

Scalable Mobile or Web Apps: Developers needing to rapidly deploy and manage applications with variable traffic might find Google App Engine most suitable.

Future Trends

The future of cloud computing with these providers will likely see an increased focus on artificial intelligence, machine learning, and hybrid cloud environments. Security and compliance will also remain top priorities as businesses continue to navigate complex regulatory landscapes. Furthermore, sustainability will become a more significant factor, with providers increasingly highlighting their commitments to reducing carbon footprints and enhancing energy efficiency.

Cloud software environments: Eucalyptus, OpenStack

In the realm of cloud computing, various software environments enable the deployment and management of scalable cloud services. Two notable platforms are Eucalyptus and OpenStack, which provide comprehensive frameworks for building private and public clouds. Each has its unique features and caters to specific enterprise needs.

Eucalyptus

Features and Strengths:

AWS Compatibility: Eucalyptus is known for its high compatibility with Amazon Web Services (AWS), allowing users to migrate applications between a Eucalyptus private cloud and the AWS public cloud without modification.

Open Source: As an open-source software, Eucalyptus supports widespread collaboration and modification, allowing organizations to customize their cloud deployments to fit their specific requirements.

Hybrid Cloud Capabilities: Supports the creation of hybrid clouds by linking private resources with AWS, providing flexibility in data deployment and scaling.

Technology Stack: Utilizes familiar technologies such as Linux, Java, and Web services, which makes it accessible for organizations with existing expertise in these areas.

OpenStack

Features and Strengths:

Wide Industry Support: Backed by major industry players like IBM, Red Hat, and Cisco, OpenStack has a robust ecosystem and a large community contributing to its development.

Flexibility and Modularity: OpenStack is highly modular, offering various components that can be independently deployed and scaled to manage compute, storage, and networking resources in the cloud.

Open Source: As an open-source platform, OpenStack allows for high levels of customization and integration with existing systems, making it ideal for enterprises that need to tailor their cloud infrastructure.

Rich Set of Features: Includes comprehensive management tools for tasks such as orchestration, fault management, and service management, which are essential for maintaining large-scale cloud operations.

Comparative Considerations

Scope of Use: Eucalyptus may be better suited for smaller organizations or those that require tight integration with AWS for hybrid cloud deployments. In contrast, OpenStack is ideal for large enterprises or service providers that need a highly scalable and flexible cloud infrastructure that can be customized extensively.

Community and Support: OpenStack has a larger support community and broader industry backing compared to Eucalyptus, which can be a critical factor in choosing a cloud platform due to the availability of support and resources.

Compatibility and Integration: Eucalyptus offers seamless integration with AWS, which is beneficial for organizations heavily invested in the Amazon cloud ecosystem. Meanwhile, OpenStack offers broad compatibility with various technologies and vendors, giving it an edge in diverse environments.

Introduction to Docker: Components, containers, images, repositories

Docker is a powerful platform designed to make it easier to create, deploy, and run applications by using containers. Containers allow a developer to package up an application with all of the parts it needs, such as libraries and other dependencies, and ship it all out as one package. This ensures that the application will run on any other Linux machine regardless of any customized settings that machine might have that could differ from the machine used for writing and testing the code.

Key Components of Docker

Docker Engine

The core part of Docker, the Docker Engine is a lightweight runtime and robust tooling that manages containers, images, builds, and more. It includes the Docker daemon (dockerd), a REST API specifying interfaces that programs can use to talk to and instruct the Docker daemon, and a command line interface (CLI) client (docker).

Docker Containers

Containers are the runnable instances of Docker images. They isolate applications from their environment and ensure that they work uniformly despite differences for instance between development and staging.

Docker Images

An image is a lightweight, standalone, executable package of software that includes everything needed to run a piece of software, including the code, a runtime, libraries, environment variables, and configuration files. Images are immutable, which makes containers based on them portable and predictable.

Docker Repositories

Repositories are collections of Docker images. Docker Hub and Docker Cloud are public registries that anyone can use, and organizations can also have private registries. These repositories allow users to share images and automate workflows.

How Docker Works

Images to Containers: Docker uses a client-server architecture. The Docker client talks to the Docker daemon, which does the heavy lifting of building, running, and distributing your Docker containers. The Docker client and daemon can run on the same system, or you can connect a Docker client to a remote Docker daemon. The Docker client and daemon communicate using a REST API, over UNIX sockets or a network interface.

Layered Filesystem: Docker images use a layered filesystem (UnionFS) that layers each file or directory change over a base image. Each modification is stored as a layer, and new containers can reuse these layers for new builds, which saves space and reduces the time to build and pull images.

Registry Interaction: When you run a container, Docker finds the appropriate image in your local system. If it's not available locally, Docker pulls it from the configured registry, such as Docker Hub.

Container Management: Once a container is launched, Docker Engine takes care of arranging the filesystem mounted to the container, networking interfaces that allow the container to communicate with the internet and other containers, and manages the application process that you want to run.

Benefits of Using Docker

Consistency: Docker ensures consistency across multiple development, release cycles, and standardizing your environment.

Isolation: Containers are isolated from each other and the host system, reducing the potential for conflicts between containers or between applications and the host.

Portability: Once a Docker container is created, it can be run on any other machine that has Docker installed, regardless of the underlying operating system.

Microservices Architecture: Docker suits microservices architecture well by allowing each service to be encapsulated in its container, with its dependencies.

Summary

Google App Engine: PaaS solution for building and deploying applications without managing infrastructure; integrates with Google services and supports multiple programming languages.

Amazon Web Services (AWS): Extensive range of services including EC2 for servers and S3 for storage; market leader with global data centres and continuous innovation in AI and IoT.

Microsoft Azure: Strong hybrid cloud solutions; integrates seamlessly with Microsoft products like Office 365; offers powerful development tools and comprehensive AI and analytics tools.

Comparative Considerations: Azure suits enterprises invested in Microsoft; AWS excels in innovation and extensive services; Google App Engine is ideal for scalable mobile or web apps.

Eucalyptus: Compatible with AWS for hybrid cloud capabilities; open-source with support for Linux, Java, and Web services.

OpenStack: Backed by major industry players; highly customizable and modular; suitable for large-scale cloud infrastructure.

Comparative Considerations: Eucalyptus is suited for smaller organizations needing AWS integration; OpenStack is ideal for flexible, large-scale cloud environments.

Docker: Containers ensure uniformity across environments by packaging applications with dependencies; benefits include consistency, isolation, portability, and support for microservices architecture.

Glossary

Google App Engine: A PaaS solution that allows developers to build and deploy applications without managing infrastructure, with automatic scalability and integration with Google services.
Amazon Web Services (AWS): Provides a vast array of cloud services, including IaaS, PaaS, and SaaS, known for its extensive global reach, reliability, and continuous innovation in technologies like AI and IoT.
Microsoft Azure: Offers hybrid cloud solutions, seamless integration with Microsoft products, powerful developer tools, and comprehensive AI and analytics tools.
Eucalyptus: An open-source platform compatible with AWS, enabling hybrid cloud capabilities and customization for specific requirements using familiar technologies like Linux and Java.
OpenStack: A modular, open-source cloud platform with wide industry support, allowing high customization and flexibility for managing compute, storage, and networking resources.
Docker Engine: The core component of Docker, managing containers, images, and builds, including the Docker daemon, REST API, and CLI client.
Docker Containers: Runnable instances of Docker images, isolating applications to ensure consistent performance across different environments.
Docker Images: Immutable, executable packages containing everything needed to run software, making containers portable and predictable.
Docker Repositories: Collections of Docker images, available in public registries like Docker Hub and private registries, facilitating image sharing and workflow automation

Exercise

Exercise 1 – MCQ

1. Which cloud service provider offers Google App Engine?

a. Amazon AWS

b. Google Cloud Platform

c. Microsoft Azure

d. IBM Cloud

2. Which of the following is a cloud service provided by Amazon?

a. Google App Engine

b. Azure Virtual Machines

c. Amazon EC2

d. OpenStack

Exercise 2 – True/ False

1. Docker containers are typically more resource-intensive than traditional virtual machines.
2. Docker repositories are public by default and cannot be made private.

Exercise 3 – Fill in the blanks

1. ____________ is an open-source cloud software platform that provides an infrastructure for public and private clouds, offering services like compute, storage, and networking.
2. ____________ is a containerization platform that allows developers to package applications and their dependencies into containers, ensuring consistency across different environments.

Exercise 4 – One-Word

1. Which cloud platform is known for its wide range of services including EC2 and S3?
2. Which cloud software environment is an open-source alternative for creating private clouds?

Exercise 5 – Small answer

1. Name two major cloud service providers and briefly describe the services they offer.
2. What is the role of repositories in Docker, and why are they important?

Exercise 6 – Long answer

1. Compare and contrast the cloud environments provided by Google App Engine, Amazon AWS, and Microsoft Azure. Discuss their strengths and potential use cases.
2. Explain the key components of Docker, including containers, images, and repositories. How does Docker streamline the deployment process in cloud environments?

Answer

Exercise 1 – MCQ

Ans: 1 b, 2 a.

Exercise 2 – True/False

Ans: 1 False, 2 False.

Exercise 3 – Fill in The Blanks

Ans: 1OpenStack, 2 Docker.

Exercise 4 – One-Word

Ans: 1 Amazon AWS, 2 Eucalyptus.

Online Resources

1. **True/False Practice Paper :** https://forms.gle/rd6fwYE8mtnJqk7a7

QR Code

2. **True/False Video Link:** https://www.youtube.com/playlist?list=PLzlh_31VWEFoq-CT06__5UwUJ37sL9vcE

QR Code

3. **One Word Practice Paper:** https://forms.gle/zjZ1BWLMwspJzhqE7

QR Code

4. **One Word Video Link:**

https://www.youtube.com/playlist?list=PLzlh_31VWEFq7NHNMTpX7TWKRLYAMZQFE

QR Code

Chapter 6: Cloud Security

Security Challenges and Issues

In today's digital landscape, security remains a paramount concern for organizations across all industries. As technology evolves, so too do the security challenges and issues that businesses face. From cyberattacks to data breaches, understanding these challenges is critical to developing effective security strategies.

1. Cyberattacks and Malware

Key Challenges:

Ransomware: This type of malware encrypts an organization's data and demands payment for its release, causing significant operational disruptions.

Phishing Attacks: Cybercriminals use deceptive emails and websites to steal sensitive information such as login credentials and credit card numbers.

Advanced Persistent Threats (APTs): These are prolonged and targeted attacks meant to infiltrate organizations and steal data over long periods.

Mitigation Strategies:

Implement comprehensive anti-malware solutions and firewalls.

Conduct regular phishing awareness training for employees.

Use intrusion detection and prevention systems to identify and respond to unusual network activity.

2. Data Security and Privacy

Key Challenges:

Data Breaches: Unauthorized access to sensitive data can lead to financial losses and damage to reputation.

Data Loss: Loss of data due to hardware failures, human error, or disasters can cripple operations.

Privacy Concerns: Ensuring personal data is handled in compliance with laws like GDPR and HIPAA is increasingly complex.

Mitigation Strategies:

Encrypt sensitive data both at rest and in transit.

Regularly back up data and implement disaster recovery plans.

Stay updated on compliance regulations and implement data governance practices.

3. Insider Threats

Key Challenges:

Malicious Insiders: Employees with access to sensitive information can intentionally harm the organization.

Negligent Insiders: Unintentional actions by employees can expose systems and data to potential threats.

Mitigation Strategies:

Implement strict access controls and regular audits of sensitive data access.

Provide ongoing security training to employees.

Use data loss prevention (DLP) tools to monitor and prevent data breaches.

4. Identity and Access Management

Key Challenges:

Credential Stuffing: Automated attacks that use stolen account credentials to gain unauthorized access to systems.

Privilege Escalation: Attackers gaining elevated access to resources beyond what is necessary for their role.

Mitigation Strategies:

Enforce multi-factor authentication (MFA) across all systems.

Employ least privilege policies and regular reviews of user permissions.

Monitor and manage session activities to detect and respond to suspicious behaviour promptly.

5. Cloud Security

Key Challenges:

Insecure APIs: APIs are often used to manage cloud services, but insecure APIs can expose organizations to attacks.

Misconfiguration: Cloud services can be complex, and misconfigurations can lead to unintended data exposure or breaches.

Mitigation Strategies:

Conduct thorough security assessments of all APIs.

Implement strong configuration management policies and tools.

Regularly review and audit cloud resource configurations.

6. Mobile and IoT Security

Key Challenges:

Device Management: Ensuring all mobile and IoT devices are secure and do not pose a risk to networks.

Data Integrity: Protecting data transmitted by these devices from interception and manipulation.

Mitigation Strategies:

Use mobile device management (MDM) and IoT security platforms to control device access and monitor for threats.

Implement robust encryption protocols for data transmitted by these devices.

Infrastructure, Data, Network, and Host Security

In the digital age, security across various IT domains is critical. Infrastructure, data, network, and host security are fundamental pillars that ensure the safe operation of all IT systems. Addressing vulnerabilities in each of these areas is essential to prevent data breaches, unauthorized access, and other security threats.

Infrastructure Security

Key Challenges:

Physical Security Breaches: Unauthorized physical access to critical infrastructure can lead to data theft or damage.

Virtual Infrastructure Attacks: Virtual environments are susceptible to attacks such as hypervisor breaches, which can compromise all hosted machines.

Mitigation Strategies:

Implement robust physical security measures such as surveillance cameras, biometric access controls, and secure data center practices.

Use secure and up-to-date virtualization technologies, and isolate critical networks and devices from each other.

Data Security

Key Challenges:

Data Breaches: Sensitive data exposure can lead to significant financial and reputational damage.

Data Loss: Loss due to hardware failure, software issues, or human error can be devastating.

Mitigation Strategies:

Encrypt sensitive data both at rest and in transit to ensure that data is unreadable to unauthorized parties.

Implement strict access controls and authentication methods to limit data access to authorized personnel only.

Regularly back up data and test restoration procedures to ensure data can be recovered after a loss.

Network Security

Key Challenges:

Intrusion Attempts: Unauthorized access attempts can exploit network vulnerabilities.

Man-in-the-Middle Attacks: Attackers can intercept and alter communications between two parties.

Mitigation Strategies:

Deploy firewalls and intrusion detection/prevention systems (IDS/IPS) to monitor and control incoming and outgoing network traffic.

Use secure communication protocols such as HTTPS and SSL/TLS to encrypt data during transmission.

Regularly update and patch network devices to close security gaps that could be exploited by attackers.

Host Security

Key Challenges:

Malware Infections: Hosts can be infected with malware, leading to data theft or loss.

Unauthorized Changes: Unauthorized software installations or changes can lead to security vulnerabilities.

Mitigation Strategies:

Install and maintain up-to-date antivirus software to detect and remove malicious software.

Implement configuration and patch management policies to ensure all hosts are consistently configured according to security best practices.

Use host-based intrusion detection systems (HIDS) to monitor hosts for suspicious activity and ensure that only authorized changes are made.

Integrated Security Approach

Security Information and Event Management (SIEM): Use SIEM tools to collect, analyze, and correlate information from different IT environments to identify and respond to security incidents.

Continuous Monitoring: Implement continuous monitoring strategies to detect and respond to threats in real time.

Security Awareness Training: Conduct regular security training sessions for employees to ensure they understand the security risks and proper protocols to mitigate these risks.

Disaster Recovery and Management

Disaster recovery and management are critical components of overall business continuity planning. These processes ensure that organizations can quickly resume operation after a disruptive event, whether it be a natural disaster, technical failure, cyberattack, or human error. Effective disaster recovery plans (DRPs) minimize downtime and data loss, helping to safeguard an organization's reputation and financial stability.

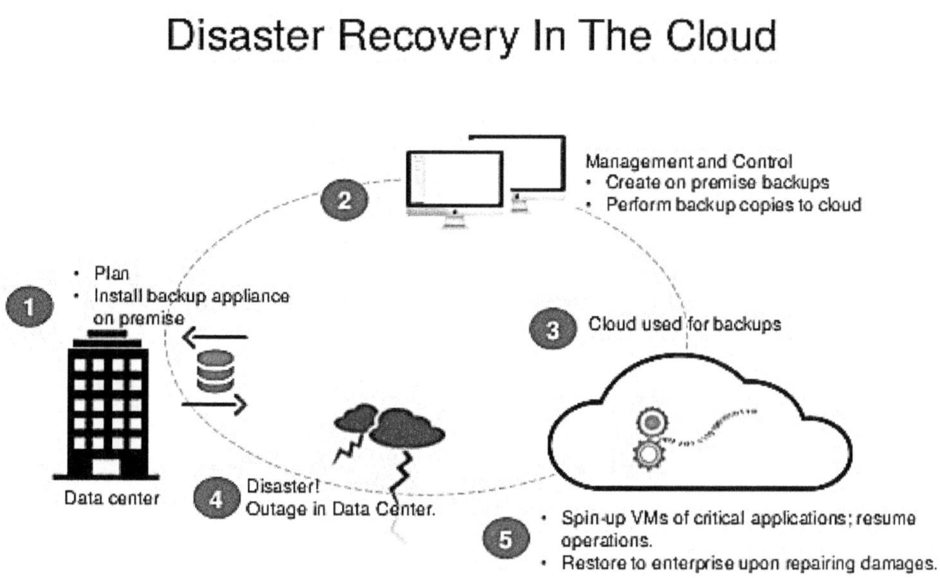

Key Elements of Disaster Recovery and Management

Risk Assessment and Business Impact Analysis (BIA)

Purpose: Identify potential threats to operations and assess the impacts disasters could have on business processes.

Outcome: Prioritize resources and recovery strategies based on which systems and processes are most critical to the business.

Disaster Recovery Planning

Purpose: Develop a comprehensive approach to recover critical systems and data after a disaster.

Components: Include detailed instructions on how to respond to various types of disasters, roles and responsibilities, recovery site locations, and necessary resources and equipment.

Data Backup Solutions

Purpose: Ensure all critical data is regularly backed up and can be restored after a disaster.

Techniques: Implement automated backup solutions that store data both on-site and off-site using cloud storage or physical storage facilities.

Recovery Point Objective (RPO) and Recovery Time Objective (RTO)

RPO: The maximum age of files that must be recovered from backup storage for normal operations to resume without significant losses.

RTO: The maximum amount of time allowed for the recovery of applications and systems to ensure business continuity.

Emergency Communication Plans

Purpose: Maintain communication with employees, customers, suppliers, and other stakeholders during and after a disaster.

Tools: Utilize multiple communication channels such as email alerts, social media updates, emergency hotlines, and mobile messaging.

Testing and Drills

Purpose: Regularly test and evaluate the effectiveness of the disaster recovery plan.

Methods: Conduct simulations and drills to practice emergency response, recovery procedures, and to train staff on their roles during a disaster.

Challenges in Disaster Recovery and Management

Complexity in Coordination: Coordinating recovery efforts across different departments and locations can be challenging.

Technology Dependence: Over-reliance on technology can be a risk if the disaster impacts digital systems and backups.

Changes in Infrastructure: Keeping the disaster recovery plan updated with changes in business operations and IT infrastructure.

Strategies for Effective Disaster Recovery

Cloud-Based Disaster Recovery: Leverage cloud computing for flexible, cost-effective, and scalable backup solutions.

Comprehensive Documentation: Maintain detailed and up-to-date documentation of recovery procedures, contact lists, and vendor agreements.

Regular Updates and Reviews: Periodically review and update the disaster recovery plan to reflect new business processes, technologies, and potential threats.

Stakeholder Engagement: Engage all stakeholders in the planning process and ensure they understand their roles and responsibilities.

Identity and Access Management (IAM)

Identity and Access Management (IAM) is a framework of business processes, policies, and technologies that facilitates the management of electronic or digital identities. With an IAM framework in place, information technology (IT) managers can control user access to critical information within their organizations. IAM systems provide a means to administer user identities and track user activities, guaranteeing that the right individuals access the right resources for the right reasons.

Key Components of IAM

User Registration and Provisioning

Purpose: Automates the process of creating, managing, and deleting user accounts and identities in various systems and applications.

Tools: Provisioning software that integrates with human resources databases to ensure that as employees are hired or leave the organization, their access to company resources is appropriately managed.

Authentication

Purpose: Ensures that users are who they claim to be when accessing resources.

Techniques: Passwords, biometrics (such as fingerprint or facial recognition), smart cards, and increasingly, multifactor authentication (MFA) which combines two or more independent credentials.

Authorization

Purpose: Controls what resources a user can access within an organization once they are authenticated.

Methods: Role-based access control (RBAC), attribute-based access control (ABAC), and other policies that determine user permissions based on specific rules.

Directory Services

Purpose: Store identity-related data and manage user information in a centralized location, making access management easier.

Examples: Lightweight Directory Access Protocol (LDAP) and Active Directory (AD).

Identity Federation

Purpose: Allows for identity and authentication sharing across different IT systems or organizations using standards such as SAML (Security Assertion Markup Language).

Advantage: Enables single sign-on (SSO), allowing users to authenticate once and gain access to multiple systems without re-entering credentials.

Challenges in IAM

Scalability: Ensuring the IAM system can scale with the growth of the organization.

Complexity: Managing the complexity and variability of IAM requirements across diverse systems and technologies.

Security Risks: Protecting against breaches that involve compromised credentials and ensuring that IAM tools themselves do not become vectors for attack.

Strategies for Effective IAM Implementation

Unified IAM Framework: Develop a comprehensive IAM framework that integrates various components such as provisioning, authentication, and authorization seamlessly.

Regular Audits and Compliance Checks: Conduct regular audits to ensure that all access rights are correct and compliant with company policies and regulations.

User Education and Training: Regularly train users on the importance of security practices related to their credentials and the risks of phishing and other attacks.

Advanced Security Measures: Implement advanced security technologies like artificial intelligence and machine learning to detect anomalies in access patterns and enhance overall security.

Best Practices in IAM

Least Privilege Principle: Ensure users have the minimum level of access necessary to perform their job functions.

Continuous Monitoring: Keep a vigilant eye on IAM tools and systems to quickly detect and respond to unauthorized access attempts.

Phased Deployment: Implement new IAM systems gradually to manage risks and allow for troubleshooting without affecting the entire organization.

Summary

Cyberattacks and Malware: Key challenges include ransomware, phishing attacks, and advanced persistent threats (APTs). Mitigation strategies involve using anti-malware solutions, conducting phishing awareness training, and employing intrusion detection and prevention systems.

Data Security and Privacy: Key challenges include data breaches, data loss, and privacy concerns. Mitigation strategies involve encrypting data, backing up data regularly, and staying updated on compliance regulations.

Insider Threats: Key challenges include malicious and negligent insiders. Mitigation strategies involve implementing strict access controls, providing security training, and using data loss prevention (DLP) tools.

Identity and Access Management: Key challenges include credential stuffing and privilege escalation. Mitigation strategies involve enforcing multi-factor authentication (MFA), employing least privilege policies, and monitoring user permissions.

Cloud Security: Key challenges include insecure APIs and misconfiguration of cloud services. Mitigation strategies involve conducting security assessments of APIs, implementing configuration management policies, and auditing cloud resource configurations.

Mobile and IoT Security: Key challenges include device management and data integrity. Mitigation strategies involve using mobile device management (MDM) and IoT security platforms, and implementing robust encryption protocols for data transmission.

Infrastructure Security: Key challenges include physical security breaches and virtual infrastructure attacks. Mitigation strategies involve using surveillance and biometric access controls, and securing virtualization technologies.

Disaster Recovery and Management: Key elements include risk assessment, data backup solutions, RPO and RTO, and emergency communication plans. Effective strategies involve cloud-based disaster recovery, comprehensive documentation, and regular updates and reviews.

Identity and Access Management (IAM): Key components include user registration, authentication, authorization, directory services, and identity federation. Best practices involve following the least privilege principle, conducting regular audits, and using advanced security measures.

Glossary

Cyberattacks and Malware: Threats like ransomware, phishing attacks, and advanced persistent threats (APTs) that disrupt operations and steal data. Mitigation includes anti-malware solutions, phishing training, and intrusion detection systems.

Data Security and Privacy: Challenges include data breaches, data loss, and compliance with privacy regulations like GDPR and HIPAA. Mitigation involves encrypting data, regular backups, and staying updated on compliance.

Insider Threats: Risks from malicious or negligent insiders with access to sensitive data. Mitigation includes strict access controls, security training, and data loss prevention (DLP) tools.

Identity and Access Management (IAM): Managing user identities and access to resources. Mitigation strategies include multi-factor authentication (MFA), least privilege policies, and session monitoring.

Cloud Security: Issues like insecure APIs and misconfiguration of cloud services. Mitigation involves thorough security assessments, strong configuration management, and regular audits of cloud configurations.

Mobile and IoT Security: Challenges include securing devices and ensuring data integrity. Mitigation involves mobile device management (MDM), IoT security platforms, and robust encryption protocols.

Infrastructure Security: Protecting against physical breaches and virtual attacks like hypervisor breaches. Mitigation includes surveillance, biometric access controls, and secure virtualization technologies.

Disaster Recovery and Management: Ensuring quick recovery from disruptions. Key elements include risk assessment, data backup solutions, recovery objectives (RPO and RTO), emergency communication plans, and regular testing and drills.

IAM Key Components: Includes user registration and provisioning, authentication, authorization, directory services, and identity federation. Best practices involve least privilege principle, continuous monitoring, and phased deployment of IAM systems.

Exercise

Exercise 1 – MCQ

1. What is a primary concern in cloud security related to unauthorized data access?

a. Vendor Lock-in

b. Data Breaches

c. Service Outages

d. Compliance Issues

2. Which type of security is concerned with protecting data stored and transmitted over the internet?

a. Application Security

b. Data Security

c. Endpoint Security

d. Physical Security

Exercise 2 – True/ False

1. Identity and Access Management (IAM) is irrelevant in public cloud environments.

2. Host security pertains only to physical security measures to prevent unauthorized physical access to the servers.

Exercise 3 – Fill in the blanks

1. ____________ is a security framework that ensures that the right individuals have appropriate access to resources, often involving policies and technologies to manage user identities and access privileges.

2. ____________ is a process that involves planning, implementing, and managing strategies to recover data, applications, and other essential IT resources in the event of a disaster or disruption.

Exercise 4 – One-Word

1. What focuses on controlling who can access information and computing resources, and tracking user activities in cloud environments?

2. What type of security is designed to protect and secure the physical and software-based resources that support storage, processing, and data transfer in the cloud?

Exercise 5 – Small answer

1. What are the primary security challenges associated with cloud computing?

2. How does Infrastructure Security differ from Data Security in a cloud environment?

Exercise 6 – Long answer

1. Discuss the role and importance of Identity and Access Management (IAM) in cloud security. How does it help in protecting cloud resources?

2. Explain the key components of a disaster recovery plan in a cloud environment. How do organizations ensure the continuity of operations during a disruption?

Answer

Exercise 1 – MCQ

Ans: 1 b, 2 b.

Exercise 2 – True/False

Ans: 1 False, 2 False.

Exercise 3 – Fill in The Blanks

Ans: 1Identity and Access Management (IAM), 2 Disaster Recovery and Management.

Exercise 4 – One-Word

Ans: 1 IAM, 2 Infrastructure Security.

Online Resources

1. **True/False Practice Paper : https://forms.gle/TyRwmw7sTcyxEKEx7**

QR Code

2. **True/False Video Link:**

https://www.youtube.com/playlist?list=PLzlh_31VWEFqW12PBx70p3tLlMs1SEwo0

QR Code

3. **One Word Practice Paper: https://forms.gle/vTgjFFzQmKtHYPSz7**

QR Code

4. **One Word Video Link:**

https://www.youtube.com/playlist?list=PLzlh_31VWEFoEPJbjyvktJmrUXMM3Nbof

QR Code

Chapter 7: Data Management and Storage

Enterprise Data Storage

Enterprise data storage refers to the strategies, solutions, and infrastructure employed by organizations to store, manage, and access large volumes of data. As enterprises generate increasing amounts of data through their operations, effective data storage becomes crucial for ensuring data availability, security, and compliance. The choice of storage solution impacts not only operational efficiency but also the ability to leverage data for business intelligence and competitive advantage.

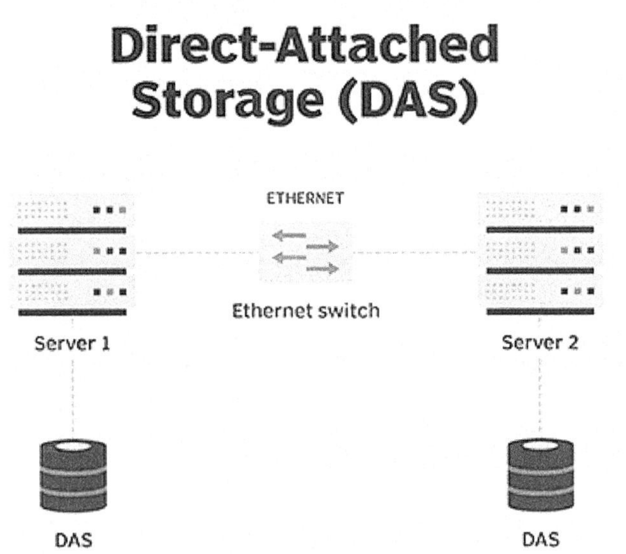

Key Components of Enterprise Data Storage

Storage Types

Direct-Attached Storage (DAS): Physical storage devices attached directly to a computer or server, typically used for single-user access.

Network-Attached Storage (NAS): Dedicated file storage that enables multiple users and heterogeneous client devices to retrieve data from centralized disk capacity.

Storage Area Network (SAN): A high-speed network that interconnects and presents shared pools of storage devices to multiple servers, making it appear as though the storage is locally attached to each server.

Storage Media

Hard Disk Drives (HDDs): Magnetic storage devices with high storage capacities, suitable for bulk storage at a lower cost.

Solid State Drives (SSDs): Faster than HDDs, SSDs use flash memory to deliver superior performance and durability.

Tape Storage: Often used for backups and archiving, tape storage provides a cost-effective solution for long-term data retention.

Data Redundancy and Replication

Purpose: Ensures data availability and integrity by replicating data across different storage devices or locations.

Methods: RAID (Redundant Array of Independent Disks), mirroring, and erasure coding are common techniques for achieving data redundancy.

Data Archiving and Backup

Purpose: Protects critical business data, ensuring it can be recovered following data loss events such as hardware failures, cyberattacks, or natural disasters.

Strategies: Implementing regular backup schedules and using off-site or cloud storage solutions to secure backups.

Challenges in Enterprise Data Storage

Data Growth Management: Handling the exponential growth of data in a cost-effective manner while ensuring quick access and data integrity.

Security Threats: Protecting stored data against cyber threats, unauthorized access, and data breaches.

Compliance Requirements: Adhering to regulatory requirements that dictate how and where data should be stored and for how long.

Strategies for Effective Data Storage Management

Tiered Storage: Implementing a multi-tier storage strategy where data is stored on different types of media based on access frequency, sensitivity, and importance. This strategy balances cost and performance efficiently.

Data Lifecycle Management: Automating the movement of critical data to high-performance storage and non-critical data to lower-cost storage.

Advanced Data Reduction Techniques: Using deduplication and compression to reduce the storage footprint and cost.

Best Practices in Enterprise Data Storage

Regular Audits and Updates: Regularly auditing storage infrastructure and practices to identify inefficiencies or vulnerabilities and updating storage technologies to meet current and future requirements.

Implement Robust Security Measures: Utilizing encryption, robust access controls, and comprehensive security policies to protect data both at rest and in transit.

Disaster Recovery Planning: Developing and maintaining a robust disaster recovery plan that includes regular testing of backup systems to ensure data can be restored quickly after a disaster.

Direct Attached Storage (DAS)

Direct Attached Storage (DAS) refers to a digital storage system directly attached to a server or workstation, without a network intervening. DAS is typically used in environments where data does not need to be shared among multiple users or systems. It is a straightforward, cost-effective storage solution suited for smaller data requirements or environments where high-speed access to data is critical.

Direct Attached Storage (DAS)

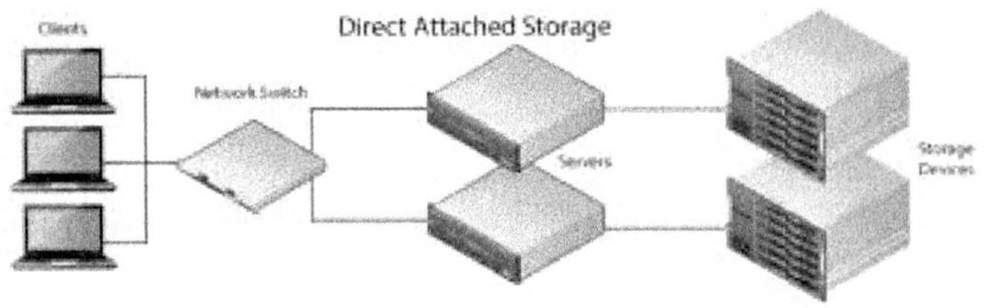

Key Characteristics of DAS

Simplicity and Ease of Use:

DAS systems are relatively simple to install and manage, requiring minimal configuration as they are directly connected to the computer or server.

Performance:

Since DAS provides a direct connection to the host computer, it often delivers faster data transfer speeds compared to network-based storage solutions like NAS (Network Attached Storage) or SAN (Storage Area Network).

Cost-Effectiveness:

DAS is generally less expensive than more complex networked storage solutions because it does not require networking hardware such as routers or switches.

Scalability:

While DAS is easy to install and expand on an individual server, scaling across multiple servers can be challenging as each device needs its own DAS system.

Types of DAS

Internal DAS: Hard drives or SSDs installed directly inside the server or PC.

External DAS: Storage devices like external hard drives, solid-state drives, or disk enclosures connected via interfaces such as USB, eSATA, Thunderbolt, or Fibre Channel.

Common Use Cases for DAS

Single User Applications: Ideal for individual users needing fast access to large files, such as video editing, graphic design, or scientific data processing.

Small Databases: Suitable for small businesses or departments that manage their database applications requiring high-speed access without the need for sharing across multiple users.

Backup and Archiving: Used for backup solutions where the data can be stored directly attached to the server and does not require remote access.

Challenges with DAS

Limited Network Connectivity: Since DAS is not designed for network use, the storage is accessible only from the directly connected server or workstation.

Data Sharing Limitations: It is not suitable for environments where data needs to be accessed by multiple users across a network.

Management Overhead: As storage needs increase, managing individual DAS across multiple systems can become cumbersome and inefficient compared to networked solutions.

Best Practices for Implementing DAS

Right Sizing:

Carefully assess the storage needs to choose the right size and type of DAS, avoiding over-provisioning and under-provisioning.

Regular Maintenance:

Perform regular maintenance and monitoring to ensure the health of the drives and to replace hardware before it fails.

Data Backup:

Implement a robust backup strategy, ensuring that data stored on DAS is regularly backed up to prevent data loss.

Security Measures:

Use encryption and secure access controls to protect sensitive data stored on DAS systems.

Integration with Other Systems:

Consider how DAS will integrate with existing systems and future needs, ensuring compatibility and ease of data transfer.

Storage Area Network (SAN)

A Storage Area Network (SAN) is a high-speed network that provides access to consolidated block-level storage, primarily used to enhance storage devices such as disk arrays and tape libraries, making them accessible to multiple servers. SANs are critical in environments where large amounts of data need to be managed and accessed quickly and reliably.

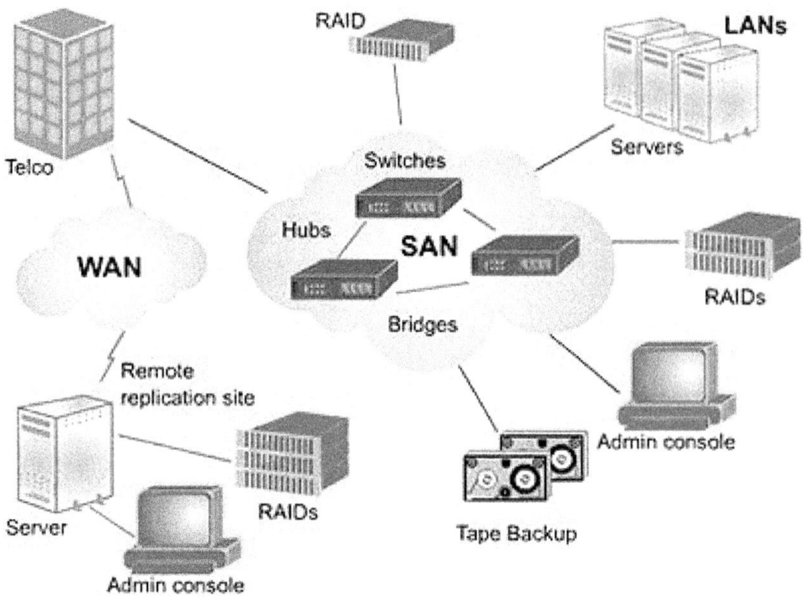

Here's an in-depth look at the key aspects of SANs:

1. Overview of SAN

A SAN is a dedicated network that connects servers to storage devices, allowing for efficient data transfer and management. Unlike traditional storage solutions that attach storage devices directly to servers (Direct Attached Storage, or DAS), SANs decouple storage from servers, providing greater flexibility, scalability, and centralized management.

2. Components of SAN

Host Bus Adapters (HBAs): Interface cards installed in servers that connect to the SAN network, enabling data transfer between servers and storage devices.

Switches: Network switches that route data between servers and storage devices within the SAN, ensuring high-speed and efficient communication.

Storage Devices: Disk arrays, tape libraries, and other storage units that provide the actual storage space for data. These devices are designed to offer high performance, redundancy, and fault tolerance.

Cabling: High-speed cabling, typically fiber optic, that connects HBAs, switches, and storage devices, ensuring fast and reliable data transfer.

3. Types of SAN

Fibre Channel (FC) SAN: Uses Fibre Channel protocol for high-speed data transfer, offering low latency and high throughput. It is commonly used in enterprise environments.

iSCSI SAN: Utilizes the Internet Small Computer Systems Interface (iSCSI) protocol to transfer data over IP networks. It is more cost-effective and easier to implement than FC SAN.

Fibre Channel over Ethernet (FCoE): Combines Fibre Channel and Ethernet technologies, allowing FC SAN traffic to be transmitted over Ethernet networks, simplifying infrastructure and reducing costs.

4. Advantages of SAN

High Performance: SANs offer high-speed data access and transfer rates, making them suitable for applications requiring rapid data processing, such as databases and virtualization.

Scalability: SANs can easily scale to accommodate growing data storage needs, allowing organizations to add or remove storage devices without disrupting operations.

Centralized Management: SANs enable centralized management of storage resources, simplifying tasks like backup, replication, and disaster recovery.

Data Availability and Reliability: SANs provide features like redundancy, failover, and load balancing, ensuring high availability and reliability of data.

5. Use Cases for SAN

Databases: SANs provide the necessary performance and reliability for database applications that require quick access to large datasets.

Virtualization: Virtualized environments benefit from the scalability and high availability of SANs, supporting multiple virtual machines and storage pools.

Backup and Disaster Recovery: SANs facilitate efficient backup, replication, and disaster recovery solutions, ensuring data protection and business continuity.

High-Performance Computing (HPC): HPC applications that process vast amounts of data in real-time rely on the high throughput and low latency of SANs.

6. Challenges of SAN

Cost: Implementing and maintaining a SAN can be expensive due to the high cost of specialized hardware, cabling, and network infrastructure.

Complexity: SANs require careful planning, configuration, and management, demanding specialized knowledge and expertise.

Maintenance: Regular maintenance and monitoring are necessary to ensure optimal performance and prevent potential issues, adding to operational overhead.

Network Attached Storage (NAS)

Network Attached Storage (NAS) is a dedicated file storage device that provides multiple users and client devices with centralized data access through a network. NAS is designed for varying scales of data storage, from small businesses to large enterprises, and is particularly effective for streamlining file sharing, simplifying data management, and enhancing collaboration across a network.

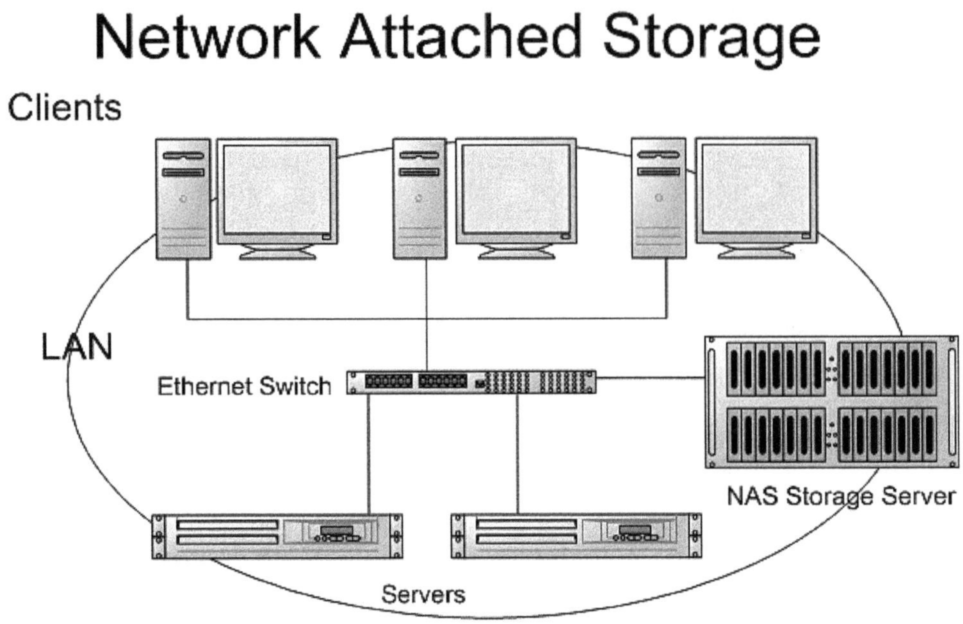

Key Characteristics of NAS

Accessibility:

NAS systems are accessible over a local area network (LAN) through standard network protocols such as NFS, SMB/CIFS, or AFP, making them versatile for different operating systems.

Simplicity:

Compared to more complex storage solutions like SAN (Storage Area Network), NAS devices are relatively easy to set up and manage, even for users with minimal IT skills.

Cost-Effectiveness:

NAS provides a cost-efficient storage solution, especially for small to medium-sized businesses, due to lower setup and maintenance costs.

Scalability:

Modern NAS systems can be easily scaled to meet growing storage needs by adding additional NAS units or expanding existing hardware.

Types of NAS Solutions

Consumer NAS: Designed for home environments or small offices, typically supporting a few drives and providing basic data backup and media streaming functionalities.

Enterprise NAS: Offers robust features designed for larger organizations, including high-capacity, redundancy, and rack-mountable solutions to support intensive workloads and a large number of users.

Common Use Cases for NAS

File Sharing: NAS systems enable file sharing across a network, facilitating collaboration by allowing multiple users to access and edit files from different devices.

Data Backup: Many NAS devices include software for automating backups, making it easy to secure data from computers across the network.

Multimedia Streaming: Home and business environments use NAS for storing and streaming multimedia content, serving as a media server.

Virtualization Storage: NAS can provide storage for virtualized environments, supporting data stores for virtual machines.

Challenges with NAS

Performance Limitations: While NAS is convenient for file sharing, the performance can be limited by network speed and the number of concurrent users.

Security Risks: As with any networked device, NAS is susceptible to security breaches if not properly secured, especially when connected to the internet.

Data Management: As data volume grows, managing and organizing data on NAS can become complex without proper data management policies and tools.

Best Practices for Implementing NAS

Network Integration:

Ensure that the NAS integrates seamlessly with the existing network infrastructure and meets the performance requirements of the organization.

Data Protection Strategies:

Implement RAID configurations to protect against data loss due to disk failure.

Regularly update NAS firmware and applications to protect against vulnerabilities.

Use strong authentication and encryption to secure data access.

Regular Backups:

While NAS can be used for backups, the data on NAS itself should also be backed up regularly to separate systems or off-site storage to ensure data recovery in case of a disaster.

Scalability Planning:

Plan for future growth by choosing NAS systems that allow easy expansion through additional disk bays or support for expansion units.

Monitoring and Maintenance:

Regularly monitor NAS performance and health using built-in or third-party tools to pre-emptively address potential failures or bottlenecks.

Cloud Data Stores and Provisioning

Cloud data stores and provisioning represent a significant shift in how data is stored, managed, and accessed in the modern digital landscape. By leveraging cloud technologies, organizations can achieve greater flexibility, scalability, and efficiency in handling their data. Here's an in-depth exploration of cloud data stores and provisioning:

1. Overview of Cloud Data Stores

Cloud data stores are storage solutions provided by cloud service providers that allow organizations to store, manage, and retrieve data over the internet. These data stores eliminate the need for traditional on-premises storage infrastructure, offering a range of benefits such as reduced capital expenditure, improved accessibility, and enhanced scalability.

2. Types of Cloud Data Stores

Object Storage: Designed to handle large amounts of unstructured data, object storage stores data as objects, each with a unique identifier. Examples include Amazon S3, Google Cloud Storage, and Azure Blob Storage. It is ideal for storing files, backups, and media content.

Block Storage: Provides raw storage volumes that can be attached to virtual machines. It is suitable for applications requiring high-performance storage, such as databases and enterprise applications. Examples include Amazon EBS, Google Persistent Disk, and Azure Disk Storage.

File Storage: Offers a managed file system that can be accessed and shared across multiple instances. It is ideal for applications needing shared file access, such as content management systems. Examples include Amazon EFS, Google Cloud Filestore, and Azure Files.

3. Cloud Provisioning

Cloud provisioning is the process of allocating cloud resources to users and applications. This involves selecting the appropriate type and amount of resources, configuring them, and making them available for use. Provisioning can be done in various ways:

Self-Service Provisioning: Allows users to provision resources on-demand through a web interface or API. This provides flexibility and speed, enabling users to quickly access the resources they need.

Automated Provisioning: Uses automation tools and scripts to provision resources based on predefined policies and triggers. This reduces manual intervention, ensuring consistency and efficiency in resource allocation.

Manual Provisioning: Involves IT administrators manually provisioning resources based on user requests. While this method provides control, it can be time-consuming and less scalable.

4. Advantages of Cloud Data Stores and Provisioning

Scalability: Cloud data stores can scale up or down based on demand, ensuring that resources match the workload requirements without over-provisioning.

Cost-Efficiency: Organizations pay only for the resources they use, reducing the need for large upfront investments in storage infrastructure.

Accessibility: Data stored in the cloud can be accessed from anywhere with an internet connection, facilitating remote work and collaboration.

Durability and Reliability: Cloud providers offer high levels of data durability and availability, often backed by Service Level Agreements (SLAs). This ensures that data is protected against loss and easily recoverable.

Security: Cloud data stores provide robust security features, including encryption, access controls, and compliance with industry standards.

5. Challenges of Cloud Data Stores and Provisioning

Data Privacy and Compliance: Ensuring that data privacy and regulatory requirements are met can be challenging, especially for organizations handling sensitive information.

Latency and Performance: While cloud providers offer high-performance options, network latency can still impact data access speeds compared to on-premises solutions.

Vendor Lock-In: Relying heavily on a single cloud provider can create dependency, making it difficult to switch providers or adopt a multi-cloud strategy.

Cost Management: Without proper monitoring and management, costs can escalate due to the dynamic nature of cloud resource usage.

6. Best Practices for Cloud Data Stores and Provisioning

Assess Requirements: Understand the specific storage and performance needs of your applications to choose the appropriate type of cloud data store.

Automate Provisioning: Use automation tools to streamline resource provisioning, reduce errors, and improve efficiency.

Implement Security Measures: Ensure data is encrypted both at rest and in transit, and apply strict access controls to protect sensitive information.

Monitor Usage and Costs: Regularly monitor resource usage and implement cost management strategies to avoid unexpected expenses.

Plan for Redundancy: Use multiple availability zones or regions to ensure data redundancy and high availability.

Data-Intensive Technologies for Cloud Computing

As businesses increasingly rely on big data analytics and real-time data processing, the need for advanced data-intensive technologies in cloud computing environments has become paramount. These technologies are designed to handle large volumes of data efficiently, ensuring that enterprises can extract maximum value from their information assets while maintaining performance and scalability.

Key Technologies in Data-Intensive Cloud Computing

Big Data Platforms

Apache Hadoop: An open-source framework that allows for the distributed processing of large data sets across clusters of computers using simple programming models. It is designed to scale up from single servers to thousands of machines, each offering local computation and storage.

Apache Spark: Known for its speed and ease of use, Spark extends the Hadoop MapReduce model to efficiently process data in-memory, making it particularly suited for applications requiring iterative computations.

NoSQL Databases

Cassandra: A distributed NoSQL database designed to handle large amounts of data across many commodity servers, providing high availability with no single point of failure.

MongoDB: Popular among developers for its flexible document model and ease of use, MongoDB is a NoSQL database that supports diverse data types and complex queries.

Data Warehousing Solutions

Amazon Redshift: A fast, scalable data warehouse that makes it simple and cost-effective to analyse all your data across your data warehouse and data lake.

Google BigQuery: A fully-managed, serverless data warehouse that enables scalable analysis over petabytes of data with a pay-as-you-go model.

Data Lake Technologies

Apache Hadoop HDFS: Hadoop Distributed File System (HDFS) is designed to store very large data sets reliably and to stream those data sets at high bandwidth to user applications.

AWS Lake Formation: Simplifies the process of setting up a secure data lake, allowing users to collect, catalog, and clean their data faster.

Stream Processing Engines

Apache Kafka: A distributed event streaming platform capable of handling trillions of events a day.

Apache Flink: Focused on providing distributed, high-performing, always-available, and accurate data streaming applications.

Challenges in Implementing Data-Intensive Technologies

Scalability: Managing the scaling of data-intensive applications and infrastructure without compromising performance.

Data Security: Ensuring the security and privacy of data across distributed systems.

Complexity: Managing the complexity of deploying and maintaining these technologies, especially in a hybrid or multi-cloud environment.

Integration: Integrating multiple data sources and types, which may require significant transformation and normalization.

Best Practices for Implementation

Start with Clear Objectives:

Define specific business goals for your data-intensive applications to ensure alignment with overall business strategies.

Focus on Data Governance:

Implement robust data governance practices to maintain data quality and compliance with regulations.

Leverage Automation:

Use automation tools for data orchestration, quality checks, and real-time monitoring to enhance efficiency and accuracy.

Invest in Skills Development:

Ensure your team has the necessary skills to manage and optimize data-intensive technologies, including training in big data analytics, database management, and cloud solutions.

Optimize for Cost and Performance:

Regularly evaluate your architecture and services to ensure you are balancing performance needs with cost, potentially using a combination of on-premises, public, and private cloud solutions.

Distributed Data Storage and Management

Distributed data storage and management have become pivotal in addressing the growing demands for scalable, resilient, and efficient data handling solutions. By distributing data across multiple nodes or locations, organizations can achieve better performance, redundancy, and fault tolerance.

Here's an in-depth exploration of distributed data storage and management:

1. Overview of Distributed Data Storage

Distributed data storage refers to the practice of storing data across multiple physical or virtual locations. This approach ensures that data is not confined to a single point of failure, enhancing availability and reliability. Distributed storage systems are designed to handle large volumes of data, providing seamless access and management across geographically dispersed environments.

2. Key Concepts in Distributed Data Storage

Replication: Data is copied and stored in multiple locations to ensure redundancy and high availability. If one node fails, the data can still be accessed from another replica.

Sharding: Data is partitioned into smaller, more manageable pieces called shards, which are distributed across different nodes. Sharding improves performance by balancing the load and allowing parallel processing.

Consistency: Ensures that all nodes in the distributed system have the same data at any given time. Consistency models include eventual consistency, strong consistency, and causal consistency, each offering different trade-offs between performance and reliability.

Scalability: The ability to add or remove storage nodes dynamically to accommodate changing data storage needs without impacting system performance.

3. Types of Distributed Data Storage Systems

Distributed File Systems: Examples include Hadoop Distributed File System (HDFS) and Google File System (GFS), which store large files across multiple nodes with high fault tolerance and throughput.

Distributed Databases: Examples include Cassandra, MongoDB, and Amazon DynamoDB, which provide distributed storage for structured and semi-structured data with high availability and scalability.

Object Storage: Examples include Amazon S3, Google Cloud Storage, and OpenStack Swift, which store unstructured data as objects with unique identifiers, suitable for large-scale storage needs.

4. Benefits of Distributed Data Storage

High Availability: Data replication across multiple nodes ensures that the system remains operational even if some nodes fail.

Fault Tolerance: The system can detect and recover from hardware or software failures, minimizing downtime and data loss.

Scalability: Easily scale storage capacity by adding more nodes without disrupting the existing system.

Performance: Distributing data and processing loads across multiple nodes enhances read and write performance, particularly for large-scale applications.

5. Challenges of Distributed Data Storage and Management

Data Consistency: Ensuring that all nodes reflect the same data can be complex, especially in real-time applications. Different consistency models offer trade-offs between performance and accuracy.

Network Latency: Data access speed can be affected by network latency, particularly in geographically dispersed systems.

Complexity: Managing a distributed storage system requires sophisticated tools and expertise to handle issues such as data synchronization, replication, and fault tolerance.

Security: Ensuring data security across multiple nodes and locations requires robust encryption, access controls, and compliance with regulatory standards.

6. Best Practices for Distributed Data Storage and Management

Implement Redundancy: Use data replication and backup strategies to ensure high availability and disaster recovery.

Choose the Right Consistency Model: Select a consistency model that aligns with your application requirements, balancing between performance and data accuracy.

Monitor and Optimize Performance: Regularly monitor system performance and optimize configurations to address bottlenecks and improve efficiency.

Ensure Data Security: Implement strong encryption, access controls, and regular security audits to protect data across all nodes.

Use Automated Management Tools: Leverage tools and platforms that provide automated management, monitoring, and scaling capabilities to simplify the administration of distributed storage systems.

7. Use Cases for Distributed Data Storage and Management

Big Data Analytics: Distributed storage systems like HDFS support large-scale data processing frameworks such as Hadoop and Spark, enabling efficient analysis of massive datasets.

Content Delivery Networks (CDNs): Distribute data across multiple locations to ensure fast and reliable content delivery to users worldwide.

Cloud Storage Services: Provide scalable and resilient storage solutions for diverse applications, from web hosting to data archiving.

Enterprise Applications: Enhance the performance and reliability of enterprise systems that require high availability and fault tolerance.

Summary

Enterprise Data Storage: Involves strategies and infrastructure for storing and managing large volumes of data, ensuring availability, security, and compliance. Key components include DAS, NAS, SAN, HDDs, SSDs, and data redundancy methods like RAID and mirroring.

Direct Attached Storage (DAS): Simple, cost-effective storage directly attached to a server or workstation. Ideal for single-user applications, small databases, and backups, but limited in scalability and network connectivity.

Storage Area Network (SAN): High-speed network providing access to consolidated block-level storage. Offers high performance, scalability, centralized management, and is suitable for databases, virtualization, and disaster recovery.

Network Attached Storage (NAS): Centralized file storage accessible over a network, ideal for file sharing, data backup, and multimedia streaming. Simple to manage and cost-effective but may have performance limitations.

Cloud Data Stores and Provisioning: Involves storing data in cloud environments, offering scalability, cost-efficiency, and accessibility. Types include object storage, block storage, and file storage, with provisioning methods like self-service and automated provisioning.

Data-Intensive Technologies: Technologies like Hadoop, Spark, Cassandra, and Kafka handle large data volumes for big data analytics, data warehousing, and real-time processing. Challenges include scalability, security, and complexity.

Distributed Data Storage: Storing data across multiple locations for high availability, fault tolerance, and scalability. Involves concepts like replication, sharding, and consistency models, used in big data analytics, CDNs, and cloud storage.

Best Practices: Regular audits, robust security measures, disaster recovery planning, tiered storage, data lifecycle management, and leveraging automation tools for efficient data management and security.

Challenges: Managing data growth, ensuring security, compliance, data consistency, network latency, and complexity in distributed and cloud environments. Addressed by implementing redundancy, monitoring performance, and using advanced data reduction techniques.

Glossary

Enterprise Data Storage: Strategies and infrastructure for storing, managing, and accessing large volumes of data, ensuring data availability, security, and compliance. Key components include DAS, NAS, SAN, HDDs, SSDs, and data redundancy methods like RAID and mirroring.

Direct Attached Storage (DAS): Simple, cost-effective storage directly attached to a server or workstation. Ideal for single-user applications, small databases, and backups, but limited in scalability and network connectivity.

Storage Area Network (SAN): High-speed network providing access to consolidated block-level storage. Offers high performance, scalability, centralized management, and is suitable for databases, virtualization, and disaster recovery.

Network Attached Storage (NAS): Centralized file storage accessible over a network, ideal for file sharing, data backup, and multimedia streaming. Simple to manage and cost-effective but may have performance limitations.

Cloud Data Stores and Provisioning: Storing data in cloud environments, offering scalability, cost-efficiency, and accessibility. Types include object storage, block storage, and file storage, with provisioning methods like self-service and automated provisioning.

Data-Intensive Technologies: Technologies like Hadoop, Spark, Cassandra, and Kafka handle large data volumes for big data analytics, data warehousing, and real-time processing. Challenges include scalability, security, and complexity.

Distributed Data Storage: Storing data across multiple locations for high availability, fault tolerance, and scalability. Involves concepts like replication, sharding, and consistency models, used in big data analytics, CDNs, and cloud storage.

Best Practices: Regular audits, robust security measures, disaster recovery planning, tiered storage, data lifecycle management, and leveraging automation tools for efficient data management and security.

Challenges: Managing data growth, ensuring security, compliance, data consistency, network latency, and complexity in distributed and cloud environments. Addressed by implementing redundancy, monitoring performance, and using advanced data reduction techniques.

Exercise

Exercise 1 – MCQ

1. Which type of storage is directly attached to a single computer without a network?

a. SAN

b. DAS

c. NAS

d. Cloud Storage

2. Which storage solution is designed to provide high-speed access to large volumes of block-level data over a dedicated network?

a. DAS

b. NAS

c. SAN

d. Cloud Storage

Exercise 2 – True/ False

1. Data-intensive technologies for cloud computing do not include technologies such as big data analytics and real-time data processing.

2. Data-intensive technologies for cloud computing do not include technologies such as big data analytics and real-time data processing.

Exercise 3 – Fill in the blanks

1. ____________ is a storage solution that connects directly to the computer or server without a network in between, typically used for individual servers.

2. ____________ is a type of storage system that allows multiple computers to access shared storage resources over a network, providing high availability and scalability.

Exercise 4 – One-Word

1. Which storage type is directly connected to a single computer?

2. Which type of networked storage provides file-level access to multiple users?

Exercise 5 – Small answer

1. What is the primary difference between Network Attached Storage (NAS) and Storage Area Network (SAN)?

2. How do cloud data stores facilitate data provisioning in cloud computing environments?

Exercise 6 – Long answer

1. Discuss the advantages and disadvantages of Direct Attached Storage (DAS) compared to Network Attached Storage (NAS) in an enterprise environment.

2. Explain the role of Distributed Data Storage and Management in cloud computing. How does it impact data availability and consistency across different regions?

Answer

Exercise 1 – MCQ

Ans: 1 b, 2 c.

Exercise 2 – True/False

Ans: 1 False, 2 False.

Exercise 3 – Fill in The Blanks

Ans: 1Direct Attached Storage (DAS), 2 Storage Area Network (SAN).

Exercise 4 – One-Word

Ans: 1 DAS, 2 NAS.

Online Resources

1. **True/False Practice Paper :** https://forms.gle/jwJHa87NYDdTs4Bt9

QR Code

2. **True/False Video Link:**

https://www.youtube.com/playlist?list=PLzlh_31VWEFqe56bntWMR1Aaczas7fcBu

QR Code

3. **One Word Practice Paper :** https://forms.gle/t12y39fU8RExciHq7

QR Code

4. **One Word Video Link :**

https://www.youtube.com/playlist?list=PLzlh_31VWEFqXlVBcF47kul2yuJq-PuOq

QR Code

Chapter 8: Cloud Solutions

Cloud Ecosystem and Business Process Management

The integration of cloud computing with Business Process Management (BPM) has revolutionized how businesses operate, offering unprecedented flexibility, efficiency, and scalability. This synergy between the cloud ecosystem and BPM enables organizations to streamline their processes, reduce costs, and enhance agility.

Here's an in-depth look at the cloud ecosystem and its impact on business process management:

1. Overview of the Cloud Ecosystem

The cloud ecosystem comprises a complex network of cloud service providers, technologies, and users that work together to deliver cloud computing services. These services include Infrastructure as a Service (IaaS), Platform as a Service (PaaS), and Software as a Service (SaaS), each offering different levels of control, flexibility, and management.

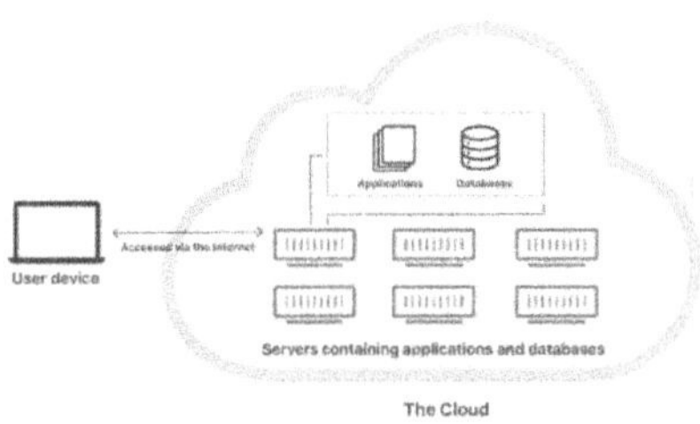

IaaS: Provides virtualized computing resources over the internet, such as virtual machines, storage, and networks. Examples include Amazon Web Services (AWS), Microsoft Azure, and Google Cloud Platform.

PaaS: Offers a platform allowing customers to develop, run, and manage applications without dealing with the underlying infrastructure. Examples include Heroku, Google App Engine, and Microsoft Azure PaaS.

SaaS: Delivers software applications over the internet on a subscription basis, eliminating the need for local installation and maintenance. Examples include Salesforce, Microsoft Office 365, and Google Workspace.

2. Business Process Management (BPM)

Business Process Management is a systematic approach to improving an organization's business processes. BPM involves designing, modeling, executing, monitoring, and optimizing processes to enhance efficiency and achieve business goals.

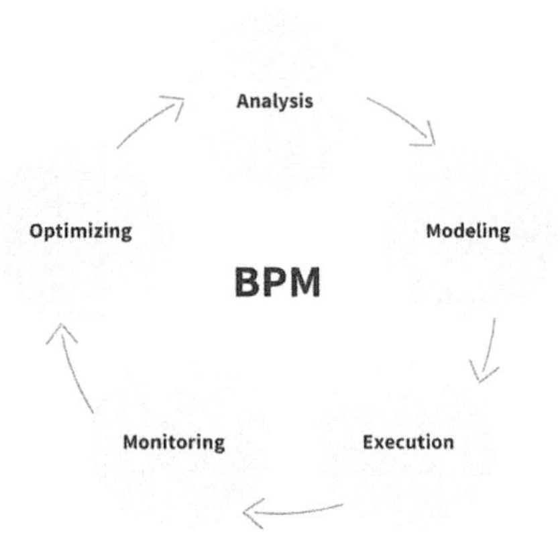

Life-cycle phases of Business Process Management (BPM)

Key components of BPM include:

Process Design: Identifying existing processes and designing new ones to meet business objectives.

Process Modeling: Creating visual representations of processes to analyse and improve workflows.

Process Execution: Implementing processes using BPM tools and technologies.

Process Monitoring: Continuously tracking process performance to identify areas for improvement.

Process Optimization: Making data-driven adjustments to processes for better performance and outcomes.

3. Integration of Cloud Ecosystem with BPM

The integration of cloud computing with BPM has several advantages:

Scalability and Flexibility: Cloud-based BPM solutions can scale resources up or down based on demand, allowing businesses to adapt quickly to changing needs without significant upfront investments.

Cost Efficiency: By leveraging cloud services, organizations can reduce the costs associated with maintaining and upgrading on-premises infrastructure.

Accessibility: Cloud-based BPM platforms provide access to business processes and data from anywhere with an internet connection, facilitating remote work and collaboration.

Rapid Deployment: Cloud BPM solutions can be deployed quickly, enabling businesses to implement and modify processes without lengthy setup times.

Integration Capabilities: Cloud ecosystems often offer integration with other cloud services and applications, enhancing the functionality and reach of BPM tools.

4. Key Cloud-Based BPM Solutions

Several cloud-based BPM solutions have gained popularity for their robust features and ease of use:

IBM Cloud Pak for Business Automation: Offers a comprehensive suite of tools for automating business processes, including workflow automation, decision management, and content management.

Appian: A low-code automation platform that allows organizations to design, execute, and optimize business processes quickly and efficiently.

Pega BPM: Provides a unified platform for developing and managing business processes with advanced analytics and AI capabilities.

Bizagi: Offers cloud-based process modeling, execution, and monitoring, with a focus on ease of use and collaboration.

5. Benefits of Cloud-Based BPM

Enhanced Collaboration: Cloud BPM platforms enable teams to collaborate in real-time, improving communication and decision-making.

Improved Agility: Organizations can quickly adapt to market changes and customer demands by rapidly deploying and modifying processes.

Data-Driven Insights: Cloud BPM tools often come with advanced analytics capabilities, providing insights into process performance and areas for improvement.

Increased Productivity: Automating routine tasks and workflows reduces manual effort, allowing employees to focus on higher-value activities.

6. Challenges and Considerations

While cloud-based BPM offers numerous benefits, there are also challenges to consider:

Data Security and Privacy: Ensuring the security and privacy of sensitive business data in the cloud is paramount. Organizations must choose reputable cloud providers and implement strong security measures.

Compliance: Businesses must ensure that their cloud-based BPM solutions comply with industry regulations and standards.

Integration: Integrating cloud BPM with existing systems and applications can be complex and may require specialized expertise.

Vendor Lock-In: Relying heavily on a single cloud provider can lead to vendor lock-in, making it difficult to switch providers or adopt a multi-cloud strategy.

Cloud Service Management and Third-Party Cloud Services

As organizations increasingly migrate to cloud-based infrastructures, managing these services effectively becomes crucial to ensuring operational efficiency, cost-effectiveness, and security. Cloud service management encompasses the tools, strategies, and processes required to manage cloud services. Third-party cloud services refer to external providers who offer additional cloud capabilities or services that complement or enhance the organization's existing cloud infrastructure.

Key Aspects of Cloud Service Management

Service Integration and Management (SIAM)

Purpose: SIAM is a methodology used to manage multiple service providers and to integrate them seamlessly to provide a single business-facing IT organization.

Benefits: It helps in creating a more cohesive IT environment that improves service delivery, enhances efficiency, and simplifies the management of multiple service providers.

Cloud Service Catalog

Purpose: This is a curated list of all cloud services available within an organization, detailing service descriptions, pricing, and SLAs.

Benefits: A service catalog helps in standardizing offerings and simplifies the process for end-users to access and utilize cloud services efficiently.

Performance Monitoring and Optimization

Tools: Utilizing cloud management platforms (CMPs) and tools like VMware vRealize, Microsoft Cloudyn, or third-party solutions like Datadog or New Relic.

Benefits: These tools provide insights into resource utilization, cost management, and operational performance, enabling proactive adjustments and optimizations.

Governance and Compliance

Purpose: Ensuring that cloud deployments comply with regulatory and corporate policies and standards.

Practices: Implementing identity and access management controls, data encryption, and regular audits to ensure compliance and mitigate risks.

Third-Party Cloud Services

Types of Services

Infrastructure as a Service (IaaS): Third-party providers offer virtualized computing resources over the internet.

Platform as a Service (PaaS): Providers deliver hardware and software tools, typically those needed for application development, over the internet.

Software as a Service (SaaS): Third-party applications are made available over the Internet.

Integration Challenges

Compatibility: Ensuring that third-party services seamlessly integrate with existing systems.

Data Silos: Preventing the creation of isolated data environments that can disrupt business processes and data analytics.

Vendor Lock-in: Reducing dependency on a single vendor, which can limit flexibility and potentially increase future integration costs.

Benefits of Third-Party Services

Expertise and Innovation: Access to specialized skills and new technological advancements.

Cost-Effectiveness: Potential reduction in costs due to economies of scale offered by third-party providers.

Flexibility and Scalability: Ability to quickly scale services up or down based on business needs.

Best Practices in Cloud Service Management and Using Third-Party Services

Clear SLAs and Vendor Management

Establish clear service level agreements (SLAs) that define the performance and service standards expected from third-party providers.

Regularly review and manage vendor performance to ensure compliance with SLAs and to adjust services as business needs evolve.

Robust Security Measures

Implement strong security protocols and regular security assessments, especially when integrating third-party cloud services.

Ensure that third-party providers comply with relevant industry regulations and security standards.

Continuous Improvement and Feedback Loops

Foster a culture of continuous improvement by regularly soliciting feedback from users and rapidly implementing necessary changes to improve service delivery.

Use analytics and cloud management tools to monitor service usage and user satisfaction, adjusting offerings as needed to better meet user demands.

Market-Based Management of Clouds

Market-based management of clouds is an innovative approach that leverages market mechanisms to efficiently allocate cloud resources. This strategy applies economic principles and models to manage supply and demand, pricing, and resource distribution within cloud environments. By adopting a market-based approach, cloud service providers and users can achieve optimal resource utilization, cost efficiency, and enhanced service delivery.

Here's an in-depth look at market-based management of clouds:

1. Overview of Market-Based Management

Market-based management in cloud computing involves using market-driven techniques to govern the allocation and pricing of cloud resources such as computing power, storage, and bandwidth. This approach aligns the supply of resources with user demand through dynamic pricing and resource allocation strategies, facilitating an efficient and balanced cloud ecosystem.

2. Key Concepts in Market-Based Cloud Management

Dynamic Pricing: Pricing mechanisms that adjust based on real-time demand and supply conditions. Examples include spot pricing, where resource prices fluctuate according to market demand, and reserved pricing, offering lower rates for long-term commitments.

Resource Auctions: Competitive bidding processes where users bid for available cloud resources. The highest bidders are allocated the resources, ensuring that resources are distributed to those who value them most.

Service Level Agreements (SLAs): Contracts that define the expected level of service between providers and users. SLAs can include performance metrics, availability guarantees, and penalties for non-compliance, influencing pricing and resource allocation.

Brokerage and Mediation: Intermediaries that facilitate the matching of resource supply with user demand, ensuring efficient allocation and utilization of cloud resources.

3. Benefits of Market-Based Cloud Management

Cost Efficiency: Dynamic pricing and competitive bidding help optimize resource costs, allowing users to pay only for what they need and use.

Resource Optimization: Market mechanisms ensure that resources are allocated to users who value them the most, leading to higher utilization rates and reduced waste.

Increased Flexibility: Users can choose from a variety of pricing models and resource allocation strategies, tailoring their cloud usage to their specific needs and budget constraints.

Incentivized Innovation: Cloud providers are motivated to innovate and improve their services to attract users in a competitive market environment.

4. Market-Based Models in Cloud Management

Spot Instances: Offered by providers like AWS, spot instances allow users to bid on unused cloud capacity at lower prices, with the caveat that resources can be reclaimed if demand increases.

On-Demand Instances: Users pay a fixed rate for cloud resources with no long-term commitment, suitable for applications with unpredictable workloads.

Reserved Instances: Users commit to using cloud resources for a specified period, often receiving significant discounts in exchange for their commitment.

Brokerage Services: Platforms that aggregate cloud resources from multiple providers, allowing users to compare prices and performance metrics to make informed purchasing decisions.

5. Challenges and Considerations

Pricing Volatility: Dynamic pricing can lead to unpredictable costs, making budget management challenging for users.

Complexity: The variety of pricing models and resource allocation strategies can be complex to navigate, requiring sophisticated tools and expertise.

Fairness and Equity: Ensuring fair access to resources for all users, particularly smaller organizations that may be outbid by larger competitors, is a significant concern.

Security and Compliance: Market-based management must address security and regulatory compliance issues, ensuring that resource allocation does not compromise data integrity or violate legal standards.

6. Implementing Market-Based Management

Automation and Tools: Implementing automation tools that monitor market conditions and adjust resource allocation and pricing in real-time can simplify management and enhance efficiency.

User Education: Providing users with clear information and tools to understand and navigate market-based pricing and resource allocation can help them make informed decisions.

Transparent SLAs: Establishing clear and transparent SLAs that outline pricing, performance metrics, and compliance requirements can build trust and ensure accountability.

Summary

Cloud Ecosystem and BPM Integration: Enhances flexibility, efficiency, and scalability in business operations, streamlining processes, and reducing costs.

Key Components:

IaaS: Provides virtualized computing resources (e.g., AWS, Azure).

PaaS: Platforms for application development (e.g., Google App Engine).

SaaS: Software applications over the internet (e.g., Salesforce).

Benefits of Cloud-Based BPM: Scalability, cost efficiency, accessibility, rapid deployment, enhanced collaboration, and data-driven insights.

Challenges: Data security and privacy, compliance, integration with existing systems, and potential vendor lock-in.

Cloud Service Management: Involves tools and strategies for managing cloud services, including performance monitoring, governance, compliance, and vendor management.

Third-Party Cloud Services: Offer additional capabilities and expertise, providing cost-efficiency and scalability, but may pose challenges like compatibility and vendor lock-in.

Market-Based Management: Uses economic principles for resource allocation and pricing, optimizing resource utilization and cost efficiency through dynamic pricing and resource auctions.

Benefits of Market-Based Management: Cost efficiency, resource optimization, increased flexibility, and incentivized innovation.

Challenges: Pricing volatility, complexity, ensuring fairness and equity, and addressing security and compliance.

Glossary

Cloud Ecosystem: A network of cloud service providers, technologies, and users delivering cloud computing services (IaaS, PaaS, SaaS).

Infrastructure as a Service (IaaS): Cloud service providing virtualized computing resources over the internet (e.g., AWS, Azure).

Platform as a Service (PaaS): Cloud service offering platforms to develop, run, and manage applications without underlying infrastructure concerns (e.g., Google App Engine).

Software as a Service (SaaS): Cloud service delivering software applications over the internet on a subscription basis (e.g., Salesforce).

Business Process Management (BPM): Systematic approach to improving business processes, including design, modeling, execution, monitoring, and optimization.

Service Integration and Management (SIAM): Methodology to manage multiple service providers, integrating them into a single business-facing IT organization.

Service Catalog: Curated list of available cloud services within an organization, detailing descriptions, pricing, and SLAs.

Dynamic Pricing: Pricing mechanism adjusting based on real-time demand and supply conditions in cloud resource allocation.

Spot Instances: Cloud resources that users bid for, offered at lower prices but can be reclaimed if demand increases.

Exercise

Exercise 1 – MCQ

1. What is the primary focus of the cloud ecosystem in business process management?

a. Integrating various cloud services to support comprehensive business functions

b. Managing cloud service costs

c. Focusing solely on data security within the cloud

d. Implementing standalone cloud services

2. What role do third-party cloud services play in cloud service management?

a. They provide additional security layers to existing cloud setups

b. They extend or enhance cloud capabilities through specialized services not provided by the primary cloud provider

c. They manage the cloud infrastructure internally without external influence

d.They focus exclusively on hardware provision

Exercise 2 – True/ False

1. Cloud Service Management does not include the management of service level agreements (SLAs).

2. Third-party cloud services refer to additional services provided exclusively by the primary cloud provider.

Exercise 3 – Fill in the blanks

1. ____________ involves the integration of cloud computing into the management and optimization of business processes to enhance efficiency and flexibility.

2. ____________ allows organizations to manage cloud services provided by third-party vendors, ensuring that they align with business objectives and deliver the expected value.

Exercise 4 – One-Word

1. Which term describes the practice of overseeing and controlling the organization's cloud services and relationships with third-party cloud providers?
2. What involves the economic and competitive aspects of cloud services, including demand and supply dynamics?

Exercise 5 – Small answer

1. What role does Business Process Management (BPM) play in the cloud ecosystem?
2. How do third-party cloud services contribute to the overall efficiency of cloud service management?

Exercise 6 – Long answer

1. Discuss the significance of Market-Based Management of Clouds. How does it influence the allocation and pricing of cloud resources?
2. Explain the concept of the cloud ecosystem. How does effective management of this ecosystem impact business processes and cloud service delivery?

Answer

Exercise 1 – MCQ

Ans: 1 a, 2 b.

Exercise 2 – True/False

Ans: 1 False, 2 False.

Exercise 3 – Fill in The Blanks

Ans: 1Cloud Ecosystem and Business Process Management, 2 Cloud Service Management.

Exercise 4 – One-Word

Ans: 1 Cloud Service Management, 2 Market-Based Management.

Online Resources

1. **True/False Practice Paper : https://forms.gle/MjP7BDjNbaSoEetR6**

QR Code

2. **True/False Video Link:**

https://www.youtube.com/playlist?list=PLzlh_31VWEFrvJHx5bQaZ6rJdlFdmltB8

QR Code

3. **One Word Practice Paper :** https://forms.gle/vyG2aUvnFTEHvpLm6

QR Code

4. One Word Video Link :

https://www.youtube.com/playlist?list=PLzlh_31VWEFrFm956-MxJfJ_GEKoudjxV

QR Code

Chapter 9: Emerging Technologies

Cloud Analytics and Testing

Cloud analytics and testing are essential components in the realm of cloud computing, enabling organizations to leverage cloud infrastructure for data analysis and ensure the reliability and performance of cloud-based applications. This section explores the key aspects, benefits, and tools associated with cloud analytics and testing.

1. Cloud Analytics

Cloud analytics involves the process of analysing data that is stored in the cloud. By utilizing cloud-based services and tools, organizations can process large volumes of data to gain actionable insights, improve decision-making, and drive business growth. Cloud analytics eliminates the need for substantial on-premises infrastructure, making it accessible and scalable for businesses of all sizes.

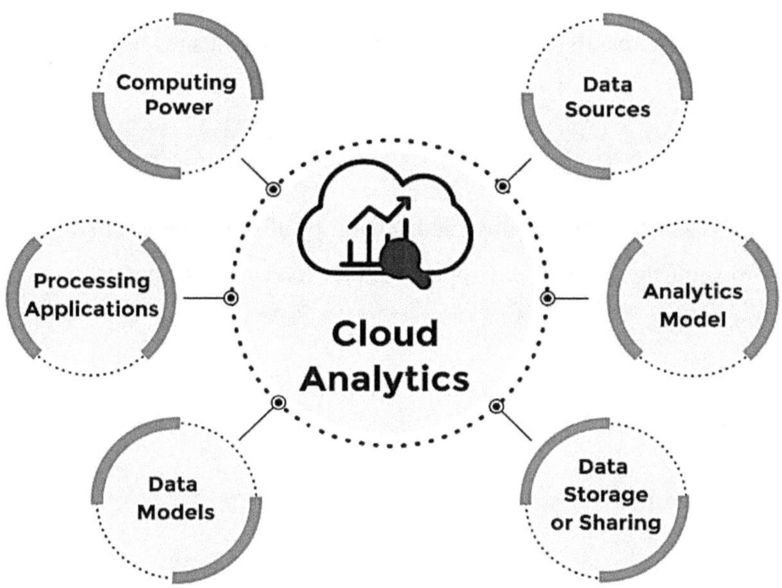

Key Features:

Scalability: Cloud analytics platforms can scale up or down based on the volume of data and the complexity of analysis required.

Accessibility: Data and analytics tools can be accessed from anywhere with an internet connection, facilitating collaboration and remote work.

Cost Efficiency: Pay-as-you-go pricing models allow organizations to pay only for the resources they use, reducing upfront costs and optimizing expenses.

Advanced Analytics: Cloud platforms offer advanced analytics capabilities such as machine learning, artificial intelligence, and real-time processing.

Popular Cloud Analytics Platforms:

Google Big Query: A fully managed, serverless data warehouse that enables super-fast SQL queries using the processing power of Google's infrastructure.

Amazon Redshift: A fully managed data warehouse service in the cloud, designed for large-scale data set storage and analysis.

Microsoft Azure Synapse Analytics: An integrated analytics service that accelerates time to insight across data warehouses and big data systems.

Use Cases:

Business Intelligence: Cloud analytics tools can aggregate and analyse business data to provide insights into sales, customer behaviour, and operational efficiency.

Predictive Analytics: By applying machine learning models to historical data, organizations can predict future trends and make proactive decisions.

Real-Time Analytics: Cloud platforms can process streaming data in real-time, enabling businesses to respond promptly to changing conditions and events.

2. Cloud Testing

Cloud testing involves testing the performance, security, functionality, and reliability of cloud-based applications and services. It leverages cloud infrastructure to simulate different environments, user loads, and scenarios, ensuring that applications perform well under various conditions.

Key Features:

On-Demand Resources: Cloud testing provides on-demand access to testing resources, allowing for flexibility and scalability.

Cost Savings: Organizations can avoid the high costs of maintaining on-premises testing infrastructure by utilizing cloud-based testing services.
Environment Simulation: Cloud testing can simulate different operating systems, browsers, and devices, providing comprehensive test coverage.
Automated Testing: Cloud platforms support automated testing frameworks, enabling continuous integration and continuous deployment (CI/CD) practices.

Popular Cloud Testing Tools:
Selenium Grid: Allows running tests on multiple machines and browsers in parallel, using the power of the cloud for scalability.
AWS Device Farm: An app testing service that lets you test and interact with Android, iOS, and web apps on real devices in the AWS Cloud.
Azure DevTest Labs: Provides environments for testing and developing applications in Azure, supporting quick provisioning and scaling of testing environments.

Types of Cloud Testing:
Performance Testing: Evaluates the application's performance under various conditions, including load testing, stress testing, and scalability testing.
Security Testing: Assesses the application's security measures to identify vulnerabilities and ensure data protection.
Functional Testing: Verifies that the application functions as expected across different environments and use cases.
Compatibility Testing: Ensures that the application is compatible with different devices, browsers, and operating systems.

Benefits:
Scalability: Easily scale testing environments to accommodate different testing needs and user loads.
Flexibility: Test applications in various configurations and environments without the need for physical hardware.
Speed: Accelerate the testing process by provisioning environments quickly and running tests in parallel.
Comprehensive Coverage: Achieve thorough test coverage by simulating diverse conditions and user scenarios.

Information Security and Virtual Desktop Infrastructure

As organizations increasingly adopt digital transformation strategies, the integration of robust information security measures and Virtual Desktop Infrastructure (VDI) solutions becomes essential. This section explores the critical aspects of information security within the context of VDI, highlighting the benefits, challenges, and best practices for securing virtual desktop environments.

1. Information Security in Virtual Desktop Infrastructure

Information security in the context of VDI refers to the implementation of security measures to protect data, applications, and user interactions within a virtual desktop environment. Ensuring information security is crucial as VDI environments centralize desktop management and data storage, making them attractive targets for cyberattacks.

Key Security Aspects:

Data Protection: Ensures that sensitive data is encrypted and securely stored within the VDI environment to prevent unauthorized access.

Access Control: Implements strict user authentication and authorization mechanisms to control who can access the virtual desktops and what actions they can perform.

Network Security: Secures the network connections between the endpoints and the virtual desktops to protect against eavesdropping and man-in-the-middle attacks.

Endpoint Security: Protects the devices used to access the virtual desktops from malware and other security threats.

Benefits of Secure VDI:

Centralized Management: Simplifies the enforcement of security policies and updates by centralizing desktop management.

Reduced Risk of Data Loss: Data is stored in the data center rather than on individual endpoints, reducing the risk of data loss from stolen or compromised devices.

Improved Compliance: Facilitates compliance with regulatory requirements by ensuring that data protection measures are consistently applied across all virtual desktops.

Enhanced Disaster Recovery: Streamlines disaster recovery processes by enabling quick restoration of virtual desktops and data from centralized backups.

2. Challenges of Securing VDI Environments

Potential Security Risks:

Unauthorized Access: Without proper access controls, unauthorized users might gain access to sensitive data and applications within the VDI environment.

Insider Threats: Employees or contractors with legitimate access to the VDI environment might intentionally or unintentionally compromise security.

Malware and Ransomware: Malware infections and ransomware attacks can spread rapidly in a VDI environment if not properly contained.

Network Vulnerabilities: Insecure network connections can expose virtual desktops to interception and tampering by malicious actors.

Addressing Security Challenges:

Multi-Factor Authentication (MFA): Implement MFA to add an extra layer of security beyond just passwords.

Regular Security Audits: Conduct regular audits to identify and address security vulnerabilities in the VDI environment.

User Training: Educate users on security best practices and the importance of following security protocols.

Advanced Threat Detection: Utilize advanced threat detection and response tools to identify and mitigate security threats in real-time.

3. Best Practices for Securing VDI Environments

Implementing Strong Authentication and Access Controls:

Role-Based Access Control (RBAC): Assign permissions based on user roles to ensure that users have the minimum necessary access to perform their tasks.

Zero Trust Security Model: Adopt a zero-trust approach where all users and devices are continuously verified before granting access.

Ensuring Data Encryption:

Encrypt Data at Rest and in Transit: Use encryption to protect data both when it is stored and when it is being transmitted over the network.

Secure Access Points: Ensure that all access points to the VDI environment are secure and use encrypted communication channels.

Maintaining Endpoint Security:

Deploy Anti-Malware Solutions: Install and regularly update anti-malware solutions on all endpoints accessing the VDI environment.

Monitor Endpoint Activity: Continuously monitor endpoint activity for signs of suspicious behaviour or potential security breaches.

Regularly Updating and Patching:

Patch Management: Implement a robust patch management process to ensure that all software components are regularly updated with the latest security patches.

Vulnerability Management: Conduct regular vulnerability assessments to identify and remediate security weaknesses.

Monitoring and Logging:

Comprehensive Logging: Enable detailed logging of all activities within the VDI environment to facilitate security monitoring and forensic investigations.

Security Information and Event Management (SIEM): Utilize SIEM solutions to aggregate and analyze log data for real-time threat detection and response.

Securing Virtual Desktop Infrastructure (VDI) is essential for protecting sensitive data and ensuring the integrity and availability of virtual desktop environments. By implementing strong information security measures, organizations can mitigate the risks associated with unauthorized access, malware, and other cyber threats. Adopting best practices such as robust authentication, data encryption, endpoint security, and continuous monitoring will help maintain a secure and resilient VDI environment, enabling organizations to leverage the benefits of VDI while safeguarding their critical assets.

Cloud Virtualization Technology

Cloud virtualization technology is a fundamental aspect of modern cloud computing, enabling the efficient utilization of physical hardware resources by creating virtual instances that can run multiple operating systems and applications simultaneously. This section explores the key concepts, benefits, types, and best practices associated with cloud virtualization technology.

1. Overview of Cloud Virtualization Technology

Cloud virtualization technology involves the creation of virtual versions of computing resources, such as servers, storage devices, and networks, within a cloud environment. This abstraction layer allows multiple virtual instances to run on a single physical hardware platform, optimizing resource usage and providing flexibility, scalability, and cost-efficiency.

Key Concepts:

Virtual Machines (VMs): Virtual instances that emulate physical computers, complete with operating systems and applications.

Hypervisor: A software layer that enables virtualization by managing the creation, execution, and allocation of resources to virtual machines. There are two types of hypervisors:

Type 1 (Bare-Metal Hypervisor): Runs directly on the physical hardware.

Type 2 (Hosted Hypervisor): Runs on a host operating system.

Containers: Lightweight virtualization units that package applications and their dependencies, sharing the host operating system's kernel but running in isolated user spaces.

2. Benefits of Cloud Virtualization Technology

Resource Optimization:

Increased Utilization: Virtualization maximizes the use of physical hardware by running multiple virtual instances, reducing idle resources.

Scalability: Resources can be dynamically allocated or scaled up and down based on demand, ensuring optimal performance and cost-efficiency.

Cost Efficiency:

Reduced Hardware Costs: By consolidating multiple virtual machines on a single physical server, organizations can reduce the need for additional hardware.

Lower Operational Costs: Automation and efficient resource management lead to lower energy consumption and reduced maintenance expenses.

Flexibility and Agility:

Rapid Deployment: Virtual machines and containers can be quickly provisioned and deployed, accelerating application development and deployment cycles.

Isolation and Security: Each virtual instance operates in isolation, enhancing security by preventing one instance from affecting others.

3. Types of Cloud Virtualization

Server Virtualization:

Definition: Virtualizing physical servers to create multiple virtual servers, each running its own operating system and applications.

Use Case: Consolidating server workloads, improving server utilization, and simplifying server management.

Storage Virtualization:

Definition: Abstracting physical storage resources to create a unified storage pool that can be managed centrally.

Use Case: Enhancing storage management, improving storage utilization, and enabling scalable storage solutions.

Network Virtualization:

Definition: Creating virtual networks that operate independently of the underlying physical network infrastructure.

Use Case: Simplifying network management, improving network efficiency, and supporting dynamic network configurations.

Desktop Virtualization:

Definition: Virtualizing desktop environments to enable remote access to desktop applications and data.

Use Case: Supporting remote work, centralizing desktop management, and improving security by keeping data within the data center.

Application Virtualization:

Definition: Abstracting applications from the underlying operating system, allowing them to run in isolated environments.

Use Case: Simplifying application deployment, improving compatibility, and enhancing security by isolating applications.

4. Cloud Virtualization Tools and Platforms

Popular Hypervisors:

VMware vSphere: A comprehensive virtualization platform offering advanced features for virtual machine management, high availability, and resource optimization.

Microsoft Hyper-V: A hypervisor-based virtualization technology integrated with Windows Server, providing robust virtualization capabilities for enterprise environments.

KVM (Kernel-based Virtual Machine): An open-source hypervisor integrated into the Linux kernel, offering high performance and scalability.

Containerization Platforms:

Docker: A platform for developing, shipping, and running applications in containers, providing an efficient way to package applications with their dependencies.

Kubernetes: An open-source container orchestration platform that automates the deployment, scaling, and management of containerized applications.

5. Best Practices for Cloud Virtualization

Resource Management:

Monitor Resource Usage: Regularly monitor the utilization of CPU, memory, storage, and network resources to identify and address bottlenecks.

Implement Resource Limits: Set resource limits for virtual machines and containers to prevent overconsumption and ensure fair distribution.

Security:

Isolate Environments: Ensure that virtual machines and containers are isolated to prevent unauthorized access and mitigate security risks.

Regular Updates and Patches: Keep hypervisors, virtual machines, and containers updated with the latest security patches to protect against vulnerabilities.

Backup and Recovery:

Regular Backups: Implement a robust backup strategy to ensure that virtual machines and data are regularly backed up and can be quickly restored in case of failure.

Disaster Recovery Plan: Develop and test a disaster recovery plan to ensure business continuity in the event of a major incident.

Automation:

Use Automation Tools: Leverage automation tools and scripts to streamline the provisioning, management, and scaling of virtual machines and containers.

Orchestration: Implement orchestration platforms like Kubernetes to automate the deployment and management of containerized applications.

Cloud virtualization technology is a cornerstone of modern cloud computing, enabling organizations to maximize resource utilization, improve flexibility, and reduce costs. By leveraging virtual machines, hypervisors, and containerization platforms, businesses can efficiently manage their computing resources and respond quickly to changing demands. Adopting best practices for resource management, security, backup, and automation will help ensure the success and reliability of virtualization initiatives, empowering organizations to achieve their goals in an increasingly digital landscape.

Cloud and Service-Oriented Architecture (SOA) Integration

The integration of cloud computing and Service-Oriented Architecture (SOA) represents a significant advancement in the design and deployment of scalable, flexible, and efficient IT systems. This integration leverages the strengths of both cloud and SOA to deliver robust services that can adapt to dynamic business needs. This section explores the key concepts, benefits, challenges, and best practices associated with the integration of cloud computing and SOA.

1. Overview of Cloud and SOA Integration

Service-Oriented Architecture (SOA): SOA is an architectural pattern where discrete software services are provided to other components over a network. Each service is a self-contained unit of functionality with a well-defined interface, enabling interoperability and reuse across different applications.

Cloud Computing: Cloud computing provides on-demand access to computing resources such as servers, storage, and applications over the internet. It offers scalability, flexibility, and cost-efficiency by abstracting the underlying infrastructure and delivering resources as a service.

Integration of Cloud and SOA: Integrating cloud computing with SOA involves deploying SOA-based services in the cloud, leveraging cloud infrastructure to enhance the scalability, availability, and manageability of these services. This combination allows organizations to build highly adaptive and resilient IT environments.

2. Key Concepts in Cloud and SOA Integration

Service Abstraction:
Definition: Abstracting the underlying infrastructure and implementation details of services, exposing only the necessary interfaces.
Benefit: Simplifies the integration and interaction between services and cloud resources.

Loose Coupling:
Definition: Designing services with minimal dependencies on each other, enabling them to function independently.
Benefit: Enhances flexibility and reduces the impact of changes or failures in one service on others.

Interoperability:
Definition: Ensuring that services can work together seamlessly, regardless of their underlying platforms or technologies.
Benefit: Facilitates the integration of diverse systems and technologies within the cloud environment.

Reusability:
Definition: Designing services to be reusable across different applications and contexts.
Benefit: Reduces development time and costs by leveraging existing services for new projects.

3. Benefits of Integrating Cloud and SOA

Scalability:
Dynamic Scaling: Cloud infrastructure can dynamically allocate resources based on service demand, ensuring that services can scale up or down as needed.
Load Balancing: Cloud platforms offer built-in load balancing to distribute traffic across multiple instances of a service, improving performance and reliability.

Cost Efficiency:
Pay-as-You-Go: Organizations pay only for the resources they consume, optimizing costs and reducing the need for significant upfront investments.
Resource Optimization: Cloud platforms provide tools for monitoring and optimizing resource usage, ensuring cost-effective operations.

Flexibility and Agility:
Rapid Deployment: Services can be quickly deployed and updated in the cloud, accelerating time-to-market for new features and applications.

Adaptability: The combination of cloud and SOA allows organizations to quickly adapt to changing business requirements and market conditions.

Improved Management:

Centralized Management: Cloud platforms offer centralized management consoles for monitoring and managing services, simplifying administrative tasks.

Automated Provisioning: Automation tools enable the automated provisioning and deprovisioning of resources, reducing manual intervention and operational overhead.

4. Challenges of Cloud and SOA Integration

Security and Compliance:

Data Protection: Ensuring the security and privacy of data in transit and at rest is critical in a cloud environment.

Regulatory Compliance: Organizations must comply with industry-specific regulations and standards when deploying services in the cloud.

Performance and Latency:

Network Latency: Communication between cloud-based services can introduce latency, affecting performance.

Performance Variability: Cloud resources can experience performance variability, impacting the consistency of service delivery.

Service Management:

Complexity: Managing a large number of distributed services in the cloud can be complex and require sophisticated tools and expertise.

Service Dependency: Understanding and managing dependencies between services is essential to ensure reliability and avoid cascading failures.

5. Best Practices for Cloud and SOA Integration

Design for Cloud:

Cloud-Native Services: Design services specifically for the cloud, leveraging cloud-native features such as auto-scaling, load balancing, and distributed storage.

Microservices Architecture: Adopt a microservices architecture to break down monolithic applications into smaller, independent services that can be deployed and managed separately.

Implement Robust Security Measures:

Encryption: Use encryption to protect data in transit and at rest.

Access Controls: Implement strong access controls and identity management solutions to secure access to services and data.
Security Audits: Conduct regular security audits and vulnerability assessments to identify and mitigate potential risks.

Optimize Performance:
Monitoring and Analytics: Use monitoring and analytics tools to track service performance and identify bottlenecks.
Content Delivery Networks (CDNs): Utilize CDNs to reduce latency and improve the performance of content delivery.

Automate Management:
CI/CD Pipelines: Implement continuous integration and continuous deployment (CI/CD) pipelines to automate the deployment and updating of services.
Infrastructure as Code (IaC): Use IaC tools to define and manage cloud infrastructure through code, enabling version control and repeatability.

Ensure Interoperability:
Standardized Interfaces: Use standardized interfaces and protocols (e.g., REST, SOAP) to ensure interoperability between services.
API Management: Implement API management solutions to govern the usage and access of service APIs.

Integrating cloud computing with Service-Oriented Architecture (SOA) offers a powerful approach to building scalable, flexible, and cost-efficient IT systems. By leveraging the strengths of both cloud and SOA, organizations can enhance their ability to respond to dynamic business needs and market conditions. Adopting best practices for design, security, performance optimization, and automation will help ensure the success of cloud and SOA integration initiatives, enabling businesses to achieve their goals in an increasingly competitive and digital landscape.

Summary

The cloud ecosystem includes IaaS (e.g., AWS, Azure), PaaS (e.g., Heroku, Google App Engine), and SaaS (e.g., Salesforce, Microsoft Office 365), providing varying levels of control and flexibility.
Business Process Management (BPM) involves process design, modeling, execution, monitoring, and optimization to improve business processes.
Cloud BPM offers scalability and flexibility, allowing businesses to scale resources up or down based on demand.

Cost efficiency is achieved through pay-as-you-go pricing models, reducing upfront costs.

Cloud-based BPM provides accessibility from anywhere, facilitating remote work and collaboration.

Popular cloud-based BPM solutions include IBM Cloud Pak for Business Automation, Appian, Pega BPM, and Bizagi.

Cloud BPM enhances collaboration through real-time access and communication, improving decision-making.

Organizations benefit from improved agility, allowing quick adaptation to market changes and customer demands.

Challenges include ensuring data security and privacy, meeting compliance requirements, integrating with existing systems, and avoiding vendor lock-in.

Glossary

Cloud analytics: Analysing data stored in the cloud to gain insights and improve decision-making. Key platforms include Google Big Query, Amazon Redshift, and Microsoft Azure Synapse Analytics.

Scalability: The ability of cloud analytics platforms to handle varying volumes of data and complexity of analysis.

Cost efficiency: Pay-as-you-go models reduce upfront costs and optimize expenses for cloud services.

Cloud testing: Testing cloud-based applications for performance, security, functionality, and reliability using tools like Selenium Grid, AWS Device Farm, and Azure DevTest Labs.

On-demand resources: Cloud testing provides flexible and scalable access to testing resources as needed.

Virtual Desktop Infrastructure (VDI): Centralizes desktop management and data storage, enhancing security and reducing data loss risk.

Information security in VDI: Involves data protection, access control, network security, and endpoint security to safeguard virtual desktop environments.

Cloud virtualization technology: Creating virtual instances of computing resources to optimize hardware usage and provide flexibility. Key tools include VMware vSphere, Microsoft Hyper-V, and Docker.

Service-Oriented Architecture (SOA): Architectural pattern for designing discrete software services, integrated with cloud computing to enhance scalability, flexibility, and cost efficiency.

Exercise

Exercise 1 – MCQ

Which technology is used to analyse large datasets stored in the cloud to derive insights?

Cloud Storage

Cloud Analytics

Cloud Networking

Cloud Computing

What does VDI stand for in the context of information security?

Virtual Data Infrastructure

Virtual Desktop Infrastructure

Virtual Device Integration

Virtual Database Interface

Exercise 2 – True/ False

Information security in cloud environments is less complex than in traditional IT environments due to the abstraction of infrastructure.

Cloud virtualization technology includes both software and hardware aspects.

Exercise 3 – Fill in the blanks

____________ is the practice of analysing data stored in the cloud to gain insights and improve decision-making processes.

____________ involves using virtualization to create multiple virtual instances on a single physical hardware platform, optimizing resource utilization.

Exercise 4 – One-Word

What is a primary focus of information security in cloud environments?

What technology underpins the creation of virtual machines in the cloud?

Exercise 5 – Small answer

What are the key benefits of integrating Service-Oriented Architecture (SOA) with cloud computing?

How does Information Security relate to Virtual Desktop Infrastructure (VDI) in cloud environments?

Exercise 6 – Long answer

Explain the role of Cloud Analytics and Testing in improving the performance and reliability of cloud-based applications. What are some tools commonly used in this area?

Explain the concept of Cloud Virtualization Technology and its impact on resource optimization and scalability within cloud environments. How does it differ from traditional virtualization?

Answer

Exercise 1 – MCQ

Ans: 1 b, 2 b.

Exercise 2 – True/False

Ans: 1 False, 2 True.

Exercise 3 – Fill in The Blanks

Ans: 1Cloud Analytics, 2 Cloud Virtualization Technology.

Exercise 4 – One-Word

Ans: 1 Protection, 2 Cloud Virtualization.

Online Resources

1. **True/False Practice Paper :** **https://forms.gle/1ougJTbvbPczrgLS9**

QR Code

2. **True/False Video Link:**

https://www.youtube.com/playlist?list=PLzlh_31VWEFoqYXHlkEuBKWDogqiRbTy9

QR Code

3. **One Word Practice Paper :** **https://forms.gle/EnqYgjPQYZpDJRwL6**

QR Code

4. **One Word Video Link :**

https://www.youtube.com/playlist?list=PLzlh_31VWEFp8GlA4R-IR_J58XR70mipj

QR Code

Chapter 10: Trends in Cloud Computing

Mobile Cloud Computing and Automatic Cloud Computing

As the digital landscape evolves, Mobile Cloud Computing (MCC) and Automatic Cloud Computing (ACC) are emerging as critical technologies, enhancing how businesses and individuals leverage cloud resources. This section delves into the concepts, benefits, applications, and challenges of these technologies.

1. Mobile Cloud Computing (MCC)

Mobile Cloud Computing combines mobile computing and cloud computing to deliver rich computational resources to mobile devices over a network. MCC enables mobile applications to utilize cloud-based resources for processing power, storage, and data management, enhancing the capabilities of mobile devices beyond their intrinsic limitations.

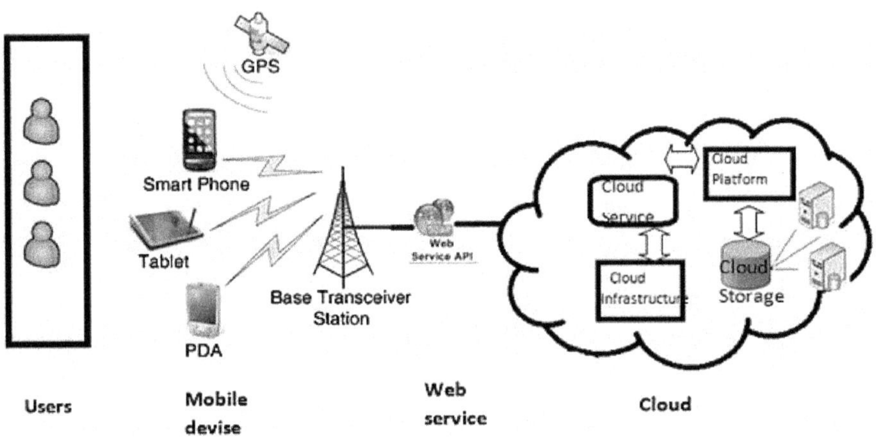

Key Features:

Resource Augmentation: Offloads computation-intensive tasks from mobile devices to cloud servers, improving performance and battery life.

Scalability: Provides scalable resources to handle varying loads and application demands.

Data Storage and Management: Offers extensive cloud storage solutions for managing and accessing data remotely.

Mobility: Ensures that users can access applications and data from anywhere with an internet connection.

Benefits:

Extended Battery Life: Offloading tasks to the cloud reduces the processing load on mobile devices, conserving battery power.

Enhanced Performance: Cloud resources provide the computational power needed for complex tasks, leading to better application performance.

Flexibility and Accessibility: Users can access powerful applications and large datasets without being constrained by the hardware limitations of their mobile devices.

Cost Efficiency: Reduces the need for high-end hardware on mobile devices, lowering costs for consumers and businesses.

Applications:

Mobile Gaming: Enhances gaming experiences by leveraging cloud servers for rendering and processing.

Mobile Health (mHealth): Supports health monitoring and data analysis by processing large datasets in the cloud.

Mobile Commerce (mCommerce): Facilitates secure and efficient transactions by handling data processing and storage in the cloud.

Mobile Learning (mLearning): Provides access to educational resources and interactive learning tools hosted on cloud platforms.

Challenges:

Connectivity: Reliance on network connectivity can be a limitation in areas with poor or unstable internet access.

Security and Privacy: Ensuring the security and privacy of data transmitted between mobile devices and cloud servers is crucial.

Latency: Network latency can affect the responsiveness and performance of cloud-based mobile applications.

Automatic Cloud Computing (ACC)

Automatic Cloud Computing refers to the use of automation technologies and tools to manage, deploy, and scale cloud resources without manual intervention. ACC leverages machine learning, artificial intelligence, and orchestration tools to optimize cloud operations, improve efficiency, and reduce human error.

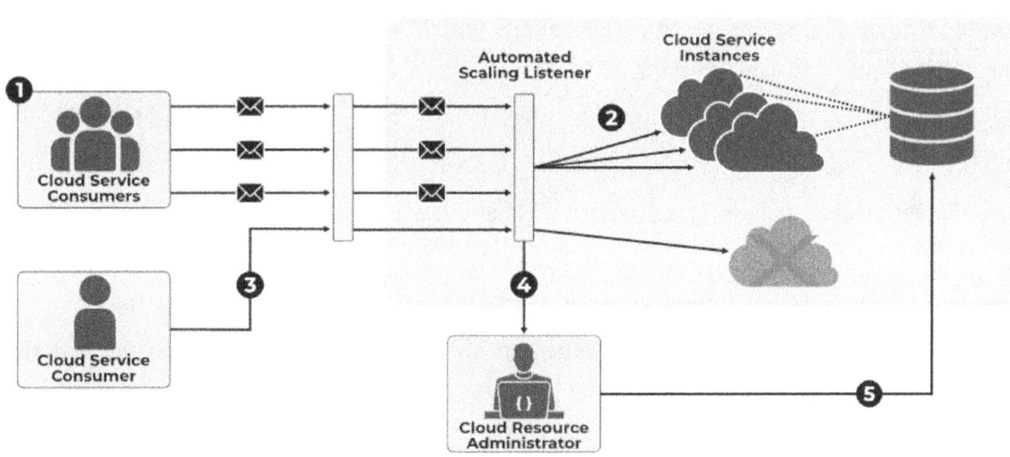

Key Features:

Automated Provisioning: Automatically allocates and deallocates cloud resources based on predefined policies and real-time demands.

Self-Healing: Identifies and resolves issues automatically, ensuring high availability and reliability of cloud services.

Resource Optimization: Continuously monitors and optimizes resource usage to improve performance and cost efficiency.

Scalability: Automatically scales resources up or down in response to workload changes, ensuring optimal performance.

Benefits:

Operational Efficiency: Reduces the need for manual management, allowing IT teams to focus on strategic tasks.

Cost Savings: Optimizes resource usage and reduces wastage, leading to significant cost savings.

Enhanced Reliability: Automated self-healing capabilities ensure that cloud services remain available and performant.

Agility: Accelerates deployment and scaling processes, enabling businesses to respond quickly to changing demands.

Applications:

DevOps: Automates the deployment, monitoring, and scaling of applications, facilitating continuous integration and continuous delivery (CI/CD) pipelines.

IT Operations: Uses automation to manage infrastructure, monitor performance, and handle routine maintenance tasks.

Disaster Recovery: Automates backup and recovery processes, ensuring data integrity and availability in case of failures.

Resource Management: Dynamically adjusts resource allocations based on real-time usage patterns, optimizing performance and costs.

Challenges:

Complexity: Implementing automation requires sophisticated tools and expertise, which can be complex and costly to set up.

Security Risks: Automated systems must be secured against potential vulnerabilities and malicious attacks.

Dependency on Algorithms: The effectiveness of ACC relies on the accuracy and reliability of the underlying algorithms and machine learning models.

Mobile Cloud Computing (MCC) and Automatic Cloud Computing (ACC) represent transformative advancements in the field of cloud computing. MCC extends the capabilities of mobile devices by leveraging cloud resources, enhancing performance, and enabling rich applications. ACC optimizes cloud operations through automation, improving efficiency, reliability, and cost-effectiveness. While both technologies offer significant benefits, they also present challenges that require careful consideration and management. By embracing these technologies, organizations can unlock new opportunities, drive innovation, and maintain a competitive edge in the rapidly evolving digital landscape.

Multimedia Cloud Applications (IPTV, Energy-Aware Cloud Computing)

As multimedia content continues to proliferate, the integration of cloud computing with multimedia applications has become increasingly significant. Cloud-based multimedia applications offer enhanced scalability, accessibility, and performance. This section explores two key areas: Internet Protocol Television (IPTV) and Energy-Aware Cloud Computing, highlighting their benefits, applications, and challenges.

Internet Protocol Television (IPTV)

IPTV refers to the delivery of television content over Internet Protocol (IP) networks instead of traditional terrestrial, satellite, or cable television formats. By leveraging cloud infrastructure, IPTV can offer a more flexible and scalable solution for streaming video content.

Key Features:

On-Demand Content: Provides access to a vast library of on-demand videos, TV shows, and movies.

Live Streaming: Supports real-time broadcasting of live events, news, sports, and TV channels.

Interactive Services: Enables interactive features such as video-on-demand (VoD), catch-up TV, and electronic program guides (EPGs).

Multi-Device Support: Allows users to access content on various devices, including smart TVs, computers, tablets, and smartphones.

Benefits:

Scalability: Cloud infrastructure can scale to accommodate a large number of concurrent users and varying content demands.

Cost Efficiency: Reduces the need for physical infrastructure and hardware, lowering operational costs for service providers.

Flexibility: Offers users the flexibility to access content from anywhere with an internet connection.

Enhanced User Experience: Provides high-quality video streaming with minimal buffering and latency.

Applications:

Residential TV Services: Delivers television services to homes, offering a wide range of channels and on-demand content.

Corporate Communications: Utilizes IPTV for corporate training, live event broadcasting, and internal communications.

Educational Institutions: Supports distance learning and e-learning by streaming educational content and lectures.

Hospitality Industry: Enhances guest experiences in hotels by providing personalized entertainment options.

Challenges:

Bandwidth Requirements: High-quality video streaming requires significant bandwidth, which can be challenging in areas with limited internet infrastructure.

Content Licensing: Securing content licenses for streaming can be complex and costly.

Security: Protecting copyrighted content from piracy and unauthorized access is a critical concern.

Energy-Aware Cloud Computing

Energy-aware cloud computing focuses on optimizing energy consumption in cloud data centers and reducing the environmental impact of cloud operations. It involves implementing strategies and technologies that make cloud computing more energy-efficient and sustainable.

Key Features:

Dynamic Resource Allocation: Adjusts resource allocation based on workload demands to minimize energy usage.

Energy-Efficient Hardware: Utilizes energy-efficient servers, storage devices, and networking equipment.

Virtualization: Reduces the number of physical servers needed by hosting multiple virtual machines on a single physical server.

Renewable Energy Integration: Incorporates renewable energy sources such as solar and wind power to offset energy consumption.

Benefits:

Cost Savings: Reduces operational costs by lowering energy bills and improving resource utilization.

Environmental Impact: Decreases the carbon footprint of data centers, contributing to sustainability goals.

Regulatory Compliance: Helps organizations comply with environmental regulations and standards.

Enhanced Efficiency: Improves overall efficiency and performance of cloud services through optimized resource management.

Applications:

Green Data Centers: Data centers designed with energy efficiency in mind, using advanced cooling systems, energy-efficient hardware, and renewable energy sources.

Cloud-Based Smart Grids: Utilizes cloud computing to manage and optimize energy distribution in smart grid systems.

IoT Devices: Energy-aware cloud computing supports the efficient processing and storage of data from IoT devices, reducing energy consumption.

Big Data Analytics: Optimizes the processing of large datasets in the cloud, minimizing energy usage while maintaining performance.

Challenges:

Initial Costs: Implementing energy-efficient technologies and infrastructure can involve significant upfront investment.

Complexity: Managing and optimizing energy consumption in cloud environments requires sophisticated tools and expertise.

Performance Trade-offs: Achieving energy efficiency may sometimes lead to trade-offs in performance, requiring careful balancing.

Multimedia cloud applications, including IPTV and Energy-Aware Cloud Computing, are transforming how content is delivered and how cloud resources are managed. IPTV leverages cloud technology to provide scalable, flexible, and high-quality television services, enhancing user experiences across various devices. Energy-aware cloud computing focuses on optimizing energy consumption in data centers, promoting sustainability and cost efficiency. Both technologies offer significant benefits but also present challenges that must be addressed to fully realize their potential. By integrating these technologies, organizations can deliver innovative multimedia services while advancing their sustainability goals in an increasingly digital and environmentally-conscious world.

Distributed Cloud Computing vs. Edge Computing

Distributed Cloud Computing and Edge Computing are two innovative paradigms reshaping the landscape of cloud computing by addressing performance, scalability, and latency challenges in different ways. This section explores these concepts, their key features, benefits, applications, and the distinctions between them.

Distributed Cloud Computing

Distributed Cloud Computing refers to a model where cloud services are distributed across multiple geographic locations but remain under the control of a central public cloud provider. This architecture enhances the performance and availability of cloud services by deploying resources closer to the users and data sources.

Key Features:

Global Distribution: Cloud resources are spread across multiple locations worldwide, reducing latency by bringing services closer to end-users.

Centralized Management: Despite being geographically dispersed, resources are managed centrally by the cloud provider, ensuring consistency and control.

Scalability: Resources can be scaled across various locations to handle increased demand, ensuring high availability and performance.

Redundancy and Failover: Geographic distribution provides redundancy, enhancing disaster recovery and failover capabilities.

Benefits:

Reduced Latency: By deploying resources closer to users, distributed cloud computing minimizes latency, improving response times.

Enhanced Performance: Applications benefit from increased performance due to the proximity of computing resources to data sources.

High Availability: The distributed nature of resources ensures that services remain available even in case of localized failures.

Cost Efficiency: Optimizes resource utilization by leveraging distributed infrastructure, potentially reducing costs.

Applications:

Content Delivery Networks (CDNs): Distribute content globally to ensure fast and reliable access for users everywhere.

Global SaaS Applications: Enhance performance and availability for Software as a Service (SaaS) applications used by a global user base.

Financial Services: Improve transaction processing times and reliability for financial institutions with global operations.

E-commerce Platforms: Ensure fast, reliable service for online shopping platforms with customers worldwide.

Challenges:

Complexity in Management: Managing a distributed cloud infrastructure requires sophisticated tools and expertise to ensure seamless operation.

Data Security: Ensuring data security and compliance across multiple jurisdictions can be challenging.

Latency in Coordination: While local latency is reduced, coordinating across distributed locations may introduce some delays.

Edge Computing

Edge Computing is a decentralized computing model that processes data at the edge of the network, closer to the data sources and end-users. This approach reduces the need to send data to a centralized cloud for processing, thereby minimizing latency and bandwidth usage.

Key Features:

Proximity to Data Sources: Processes data near the source, such as IoT devices, sensors, and local servers.

Decentralized Processing: Distributes computing tasks across various edge nodes, reducing the load on centralized cloud infrastructure.

Real-Time Processing: Enables real-time data processing and decision-making by eliminating the need to transmit data to the cloud.

Scalability: Scales horizontally by adding more edge nodes to handle increased data volumes and processing needs.

Benefits:

Ultra-Low Latency: Reduces latency by processing data locally, making it ideal for time-sensitive applications.

Bandwidth Optimization: Decreases the amount of data transmitted to the central cloud, reducing bandwidth usage and costs.

Enhanced Security: Keeps sensitive data closer to its source, reducing the risk of data breaches during transmission.

Improved Reliability: Ensures continuous operation even if the central cloud is unavailable, as edge nodes can operate independently.

Applications:

IoT Applications: Supports real-time processing and analytics for Internet of Things (IoT) devices, such as smart home systems and industrial sensors.

Autonomous Vehicles: Processes data locally for real-time decision-making in self-driving cars and drones.

Healthcare: Enables real-time monitoring and analysis of patient data from wearable devices and medical sensors.

Retail: Enhances customer experiences with real-time data processing for personalized services and inventory management.

Challenges:

Management Complexity: Managing a large number of distributed edge nodes can be complex and resource-intensive.

Security Risks: Ensuring robust security for numerous edge devices can be challenging, as they may be more vulnerable to attacks.

Data Consistency: Maintaining data consistency and synchronization across edge and central cloud locations can be difficult.

Comparison Between Distributed Cloud Computing and Edge Computing

Architecture:

Distributed Cloud Computing: Centralized management of globally distributed resources under a single cloud provider.

Edge Computing: Decentralized processing closer to data sources and users, with local management of edge nodes.

Latency and Performance:

Distributed Cloud Computing: Reduces latency by deploying resources closer to users but still relies on a central cloud.

Edge Computing: Minimizes latency further by processing data at the edge, ideal for real-time applications.

Scalability:

Distributed Cloud Computing: Scales by adding resources across multiple global locations.

Edge Computing: Scales by adding more edge nodes, enhancing local processing capabilities.

Security:

Distributed Cloud Computing: Centralized control helps maintain consistent security policies, but data travels over the internet.

Edge Computing: Enhances security by keeping data local, but securing numerous edge devices can be challenging.

Use Cases:

Distributed Cloud Computing: Suitable for global applications requiring high availability and performance across multiple regions.

Edge Computing: Ideal for real-time, low-latency applications where immediate data processing is critical.

Distributed Cloud Computing and Edge Computing both address the need for improved performance, scalability, and latency reduction, but they do so in different ways. Distributed Cloud Computing enhances the global reach and availability of cloud services by deploying resources across multiple locations while maintaining centralized control. Edge Computing brings processing power closer to data sources, enabling real-time decision-making and reducing the load on central cloud infrastructure. By understanding the distinctions and benefits of each approach, organizations can choose the right strategy to meet their specific needs and leverage the full potential of cloud technologies in an increasingly interconnected world.

Containers, Docker, Kubernetes, and Introduction to DevOps

As software development and IT operations evolve, the adoption of containers, orchestration tools like Kubernetes, and methodologies such as DevOps has become essential for building scalable, efficient, and reliable applications. This section explores the key concepts, benefits, and practices associated with containers, Docker, Kubernetes, and DevOps.

Containers

Containers are lightweight, portable, and self-sufficient units that package an application and its dependencies, enabling it to run consistently across different computing environments. Unlike traditional virtualization, containers share the host operating system's kernel, which makes them more efficient and faster to start.

Key Features:

Isolation: Each container operates in its own isolated environment, ensuring that applications do not interfere with each other.

Portability: Containers can run on any system that supports containerization, making them ideal for multi-cloud and hybrid-cloud environments.

Efficiency: Containers are lightweight and use fewer resources compared to virtual machines (VMs) because they share the host OS kernel.

Consistency: By bundling the application with its dependencies, containers ensure that the application runs consistently across different environments.

Benefits:

Rapid Deployment: Containers can be quickly deployed and scaled, accelerating the development and deployment process.

Improved Resource Utilization: Containers make efficient use of system resources, allowing more applications to run on a single host.

Simplified Management: Containers streamline the management of application dependencies and environment configurations.

Use Cases:

Microservices: Containers are ideal for building and deploying microservices, where each service runs in its own container.

Continuous Integration/Continuous Deployment (CI/CD): Containers facilitate CI/CD pipelines by ensuring consistent application environments across development, testing, and production.

Docker

Docker is a platform that simplifies the creation, deployment, and management of containers. It provides tools and features that make it easy for developers to package applications into containers and manage their lifecycle.

Key Features:

Docker Engine: The core component that enables containerization and manages the lifecycle of containers.

Docker Images: Read-only templates used to create containers, containing the application and its dependencies.

Docker Hub: A cloud-based repository for storing and sharing Docker images.

Docker Compose: A tool for defining and running multi-container Docker applications using a YAML file.

Benefits:

Simplified Deployment: Docker automates the deployment process, making it easier to distribute and run applications.

Version Control: Docker images can be versioned, allowing developers to track changes and roll back to previous versions if needed.

Scalability: Docker makes it easy to scale applications by running multiple container instances.

Use Cases:

Development Environments: Docker allows developers to create consistent development environments, reducing the "it works on my machine" problem.

Application Modernization: Docker can containerize legacy applications, making them easier to deploy and manage.

Kubernetes

Kubernetes, often abbreviated as K8s, is an open-source container orchestration platform that automates the deployment, scaling, and management of containerized applications. It provides a robust framework for running distributed systems resiliently.

Key Features:

Automated Deployment and Scaling: Kubernetes can automatically deploy and scale containerized applications based on demand.

Self-Healing: Kubernetes monitors the health of containers and replaces failed containers to ensure application availability.

Service Discovery and Load Balancing: Kubernetes provides built-in service discovery and load balancing to distribute traffic across containers.

Declarative Configuration: Kubernetes uses declarative configurations (YAML or JSON files) to manage infrastructure and applications.

Benefits:

High Availability: Kubernetes ensures high availability and fault tolerance for applications by automatically managing container lifecycles.

Resource Optimization: Kubernetes optimizes the use of computing resources by efficiently scheduling containers on available nodes.

Extensibility: Kubernetes supports a wide range of plugins and integrations, making it highly extensible and adaptable to various needs.

Use Cases:

Microservices Architecture: Kubernetes is ideal for deploying and managing microservices, providing the necessary orchestration and scalability.

CI/CD Pipelines: Kubernetes automates the deployment and scaling of applications, making it a key component of CI/CD pipelines.

Hybrid Cloud and Multi-Cloud Deployments: Kubernetes can manage workloads across different cloud providers and on-premises environments.

Introduction to DevOps

DevOps is a cultural and methodological approach that integrates software development (Dev) and IT operations (Ops) to improve collaboration, efficiency, and the delivery of high-quality software. DevOps aims to shorten the development lifecycle, increase deployment frequency, and ensure reliable releases.

Key Principles:

Collaboration and Communication: DevOps fosters close collaboration between development and operations teams to streamline processes and improve efficiency.

Automation: DevOps emphasizes the automation of repetitive tasks, including testing, deployment, and infrastructure management.

Continuous Integration/Continuous Deployment (CI/CD): CI/CD practices ensure that code changes are automatically tested and deployed, enabling faster and more reliable releases.

Monitoring and Feedback: Continuous monitoring and feedback loops help identify and address issues quickly, improving the overall quality of software.

Benefits:

Faster Time to Market: DevOps accelerates the development and deployment process, allowing organizations to deliver features and updates more rapidly.

Improved Quality: Automated testing and continuous monitoring help ensure that software is reliable and meets quality standards.

Increased Efficiency: Automation reduces manual effort and minimizes errors, improving operational efficiency.

Enhanced Collaboration: DevOps breaks down silos between teams, fostering a culture of collaboration and shared responsibility.

Use Cases:

Software Development: DevOps practices are widely adopted in software development to improve the speed and quality of releases.

Infrastructure as Code (IaC): DevOps leverages IaC to automate the provisioning and management of infrastructure, ensuring consistency and scalability.

Incident Management: DevOps practices, such as continuous monitoring and automated alerting, help quickly identify and resolve incidents.

Containers, Docker, Kubernetes, and DevOps are transformative technologies and methodologies that are reshaping the software development and IT operations landscape. Containers provide a lightweight and portable way to run applications consistently across environments. Docker simplifies container management, while Kubernetes offers robust orchestration capabilities for deploying and managing containerized applications at scale. DevOps integrates development and operations to enhance collaboration, efficiency, and the quality of software delivery. Together, these technologies and practices enable organizations to build, deploy, and manage applications more effectively, driving innovation and competitiveness in the digital age.

Summary

Mobile Cloud Computing (MCC) combines mobile and cloud computing to enhance mobile device capabilities by utilizing cloud resources for processing, storage, and data management.

Benefits of MCC include extended battery life, enhanced performance, flexibility, accessibility, and cost efficiency.

Applications of MCC include mobile gaming, mobile health (mHealth), mobile commerce (mCommerce), and mobile learning (mLearning).

Automatic Cloud Computing (ACC) uses automation technologies to manage, deploy, and scale cloud resources without manual intervention, improving efficiency and reliability.

Benefits of ACC include operational efficiency, cost savings, enhanced reliability, and agility.

Applications of ACC include DevOps, IT operations, disaster recovery, and resource management.

Multimedia Cloud Applications, such as IPTV, offer scalable, flexible, and high-quality streaming services by leveraging cloud infrastructure.

Energy-Aware Cloud Computing focuses on optimizing energy consumption in cloud data centers, promoting sustainability and cost efficiency.

Distributed Cloud Computing deploys cloud services across multiple locations to reduce latency and enhance performance, while Edge Computing processes data closer to the source for real-time decision-making.

Glossary

Mobile Cloud Computing (MCC): Combines mobile and cloud computing to deliver rich computational resources to mobile devices over a network. Key Features: Resource augmentation, scalability, data storage, mobility.

Benefits: Extended battery life, enhanced performance, flexibility, cost efficiency. Applications: Mobile gaming, mHealth, mCommerce, mLearning. Challenges: Connectivity, security, latency.

Automatic Cloud Computing (ACC): Uses automation technologies to manage, deploy, and scale cloud resources without manual intervention. Key Features: Automated provisioning, self-healing, resource optimization, scalability. Benefits: Operational efficiency, cost savings, enhanced reliability, agility. Applications: DevOps, IT operations, disaster recovery, resource management. Challenges: Complexity, security risks, dependency on algorithms.

Internet Protocol Television (IPTV): Delivery of television content over Internet Protocol networks. Key Features: On-demand content, live streaming, interactive services, multi-device support. Benefits: Scalability, cost efficiency, flexibility, enhanced user experience. Applications: Residential TV services, corporate communications, educational institutions, hospitality. Challenges: Bandwidth requirements, content licensing, security.

Energy-Aware Cloud Computing: Optimizes energy consumption in cloud data centers to reduce environmental impact. Key Features: Dynamic resource allocation, energy-efficient hardware, virtualization, renewable energy integration. Benefits: Cost savings, reduced environmental impact, regulatory compliance, enhanced efficiency. Applications: Green data centers, cloud-based smart grids, IoT devices, big data analytics. Challenges: Initial costs, complexity, performance trade-offs.

Distributed Cloud Computing: Distributes cloud services across multiple geographic locations while maintaining centralized management. Key Features: Global distribution, centralized management, scalability, redundancy. Benefits: Reduced latency, enhanced performance, high availability, cost efficiency. Applications: CDNs, global SaaS applications, financial services, e-commerce platforms. Challenges: Management complexity, data security, coordination latency.

Edge Computing: Processes data at the edge of the network, closer to data sources and end-users. Key Features: Proximity to data sources, decentralized processing, real-time processing, scalability. Benefits: Ultra-low latency, bandwidth optimization, enhanced security, improved reliability. Applications: IoT applications, autonomous vehicles, healthcare, retail. Challenges: Management complexity, security risks, data consistency.

Containers: Lightweight, portable units that package an application and its dependencies. Key Features: Isolation, portability, efficiency, consistency. Benefits: Rapid deployment, improved resource utilization, simplified management. Applications: Microservices, CI/CD pipelines.

Docker: A platform for creating, deploying, and managing containers. Key Features: Docker Engine, Docker images, Docker Hub, Docker Compose. Benefits: Simplified deployment, version control, scalability. Applications: Development environments, application modernization.

Kubernetes: An open-source container orchestration platform that automates the deployment, scaling, and management of containerized applications. Key Features: Automated deployment, self-healing, service discovery, declarative configuration. Benefits: High availability, resource optimization, extensibility. Applications: Microservices architecture, CI/CD pipelines, hybrid cloud deployments.

DevOps: Integrates software development (Dev) and IT operations (Ops) to improve collaboration and efficiency. Key Principles: Collaboration, automation, CI/CD, monitoring and feedback. Benefits: Faster time to market, improved quality, increased efficiency, enhanced collaboration. Applications: Software development, infrastructure as code, incident management.

Exercise

Exercise 1 – MCQ

Which technology is primarily associated with automating the deployment, scaling, and management of containerized applications?

Docker

Kubernetes

Edge Computing

IPTV

Which of the following is a key feature of Automatic Cloud Computing (ACC)?

Manual provisioning of cloud resources

Self-healing capabilities

High reliance on physical servers

Local data processing on edge devices

Exercise 2 – True/ False

Multimedia cloud applications, like IPTV, do not consume significant energy, thus energy-aware cloud computing is not necessary for them.

Distributed cloud computing and edge computing are the same, with both terms referring to processing data on edge devices.

Exercise 3 – Fill in the blanks

____________ is a paradigm that brings computing power closer to data sources, reducing latency by processing data locally, often used in applications like autonomous vehicles.

____________ is an orchestration tool that automates the deployment, scaling, and management of containerized applications, often used in DevOps practices.

Exercise 4 – One-Word

Which is a system for automating the deployment, scaling, and management of containerized applications?

Which cloud application involves delivering multimedia content such as television over internet protocols directly through cloud services

Exercise 5 – Small answer

What is the main difference between Distributed Cloud Computing and Edge Computing in terms of data processing location?

How does Energy-Aware Cloud Computing contribute to sustainability in cloud operations?

Exercise 6 – Long answer

Discuss the advantages and challenges of Mobile Cloud Computing. How does it enhance the capabilities of mobile devices?

Explain the role of Containers, Docker, and Kubernetes in modern DevOps practices. How do they work together to streamline application development and deployment?

Answer

Exercise 1 – MCQ

Ans: 1 b, 2 b.

Exercise 2 – True/False

Ans: 1 False, 2 False.

Exercise 3 – Fill in The Blanks

Ans: 1Edge Computing, 2 Kubernetes.

Exercise 4 – One-Word

Ans: 1 IPTV, 2 Kubernetes.

Online Resources

1. **True/False Practice Paper : https://forms.gle/1SjfeZWxaRWTNh8r5**

QR Code

2. **True/False Video Link :**

https://www.youtube.com/playlist?list=PLzlh_31VWEFqWQ4s4BJ2DPMCcb4RoeUWg

QR Code

3. **One Word Practice Paper : https://forms.gle/Hh1QsSKGep8YAELCA**

QR Code

4. One Word Video Link :

https://www.youtube.com/playlist?list=PLzlh_31VWEFqkJQc9mIW4yDlUK6HAr_P_

QR Code

Chapter 11: IoT and Cloud Convergence

IoT Categories and Characteristics

The Internet of Things (IoT) represents a paradigm shift in how devices, systems, and services interact and share data. IoT encompasses a wide range of applications, each with distinct characteristics and requirements. This section explores the various categories of IoT and their defining characteristics.

IoT Categories

Consumer IoT: Consumer IoT encompasses devices and applications used by individuals in their daily lives. These devices are often connected to personal networks and the internet, providing convenience, automation, and enhanced user experiences.

Key Examples:

Smart Homes: Devices like smart thermostats, smart lighting systems, and home security cameras that can be controlled remotely via smartphones or voice assistants.

Wearables: Fitness trackers, smartwatches, and health monitoring devices that track physical activity, health metrics, and provide notifications.

Smart Appliances: Internet-connected refrigerators, washing machines, and coffee makers that can be controlled and monitored remotely.

Industrial IoT (IIoT): Industrial IoT refers to the use of IoT technologies in industrial applications to enhance operational efficiency, productivity, and safety. IIoT connects machines, sensors, and devices in manufacturing, energy, and other industrial sectors.

Key Examples:

Smart Factories: Automated production lines with connected machinery and sensors that monitor performance and optimize operations.

Predictive Maintenance: Sensors on industrial equipment that collect data to predict failures and schedule maintenance before breakdowns occur.

Supply Chain Management: IoT-enabled tracking of goods and inventory in real-time to optimize logistics and reduce losses.

Healthcare IoT: Healthcare IoT involves the use of connected devices to monitor patients, manage chronic diseases, and improve healthcare delivery. These devices collect and transmit health data to healthcare providers for analysis and intervention.

Key Examples:

Remote Patient Monitoring: Wearable devices that track vital signs and transmit data to healthcare providers for remote monitoring.
Smart Medical Devices: Connected insulin pumps, inhalers, and other medical devices that provide real-time data and alerts.
Telemedicine: Platforms that enable remote consultations and diagnostics using IoT devices and communication technologies.

Smart Cities: Smart cities leverage IoT technologies to improve urban infrastructure, enhance public services, and create sustainable environments. IoT solutions in smart cities aim to optimize resource use, reduce costs, and improve the quality of life for residents.

Key Examples:
Smart Transportation: Connected traffic lights, public transportation systems, and smart parking solutions that improve traffic flow and reduce congestion.
Environmental Monitoring: Sensors that monitor air quality, noise levels, and water quality to ensure a healthy urban environment.
Smart Grids: IoT-enabled electricity grids that optimize energy distribution, reduce outages, and integrate renewable energy sources.

Agricultural IoT: Agricultural IoT, or smart farming, uses IoT technologies to enhance agricultural productivity and sustainability. These solutions monitor and manage crops, livestock, and farming operations.

Key Examples:
Precision Agriculture: Sensors and drones that collect data on soil conditions, weather, and crop health to optimize farming practices.
Livestock Monitoring: Wearable devices for livestock that track health metrics, location, and behavior to improve animal welfare and productivity.
Smart Irrigation: IoT-enabled irrigation systems that adjust watering schedules based on real-time soil moisture and weather data.

Characteristics of IoT

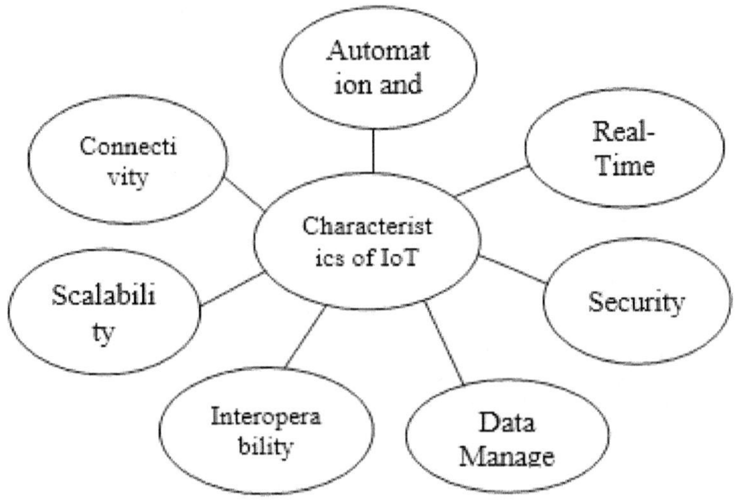

Connectivity: IoT devices rely on robust connectivity to transmit data to other devices, networks, or cloud platforms. Connectivity options include Wi-Fi, Bluetooth, Zigbee, LoRaWAN, and cellular networks. Reliable connectivity is crucial for the real-time exchange of information and the seamless functioning of IoT systems.

Scalability: IoT systems must be scalable to handle the increasing number of connected devices and the growing volume of data they generate. Scalability ensures that IoT solutions can expand and adapt to meet evolving demands without compromising performance.

Interoperability: Interoperability refers to the ability of IoT devices and systems to work together, regardless of manufacturer or protocol. Standardization and common communication protocols are essential to achieve interoperability, enabling diverse devices to share and interpret data effectively.

Data Management: IoT generates vast amounts of data that need to be collected, processed, stored, and analysed. Effective data management practices ensure that relevant insights are derived from the data, supporting decision-making and automation. This involves using cloud platforms, edge computing, and data analytics tools.

Security: Security is a critical characteristic of IoT, as connected devices can be vulnerable to cyberattacks. Implementing robust security measures, such as encryption, authentication, and access control, protects data integrity and privacy. Regular updates and security patches are also necessary to mitigate risks.

Real-Time Processing: Many IoT applications require real-time data processing to provide immediate insights and responses. Real-time processing is essential for applications like autonomous vehicles, healthcare monitoring, and industrial automation, where timely decision-making is crucial.

Automation and Intelligence: IoT systems often incorporate automation and intelligence to enhance functionality and efficiency. Automation involves using IoT devices to perform tasks without human intervention, while intelligence leverages artificial intelligence (AI) and machine learning (ML) to analyse data and make predictive or autonomous decisions.

The Internet of Things (IoT) encompasses a wide range of applications across various sectors, each with distinct characteristics and benefits. From consumer IoT and industrial IoT to healthcare, smart cities, and agriculture, IoT technologies are transforming how we live and work. Understanding the key characteristics of IoT, such as connectivity, scalability, interoperability, data management, security, real-time processing, and automation, is essential for developing and deploying effective IoT solutions. As IoT continues to evolve, it will play an increasingly important role in driving innovation, efficiency, and sustainability in diverse domains.

Connectivity Technologies (RFID, NFC, Bluetooth, etc.)

Connectivity technologies are fundamental to the Internet of Things (IoT), enabling communication between devices and the exchange of data across networks. This section explores various connectivity technologies, including RFID, NFC, Bluetooth, Wi-Fi, Zigbee, and LoRaWAN, highlighting their features, applications, and advantages.

1. Radio Frequency Identification (RFID)

RFID uses electromagnetic fields to automatically identify and track tags attached to objects. RFID systems consist of a reader, an antenna, and RFID tags, which can be active (battery-powered) or passive (powered by the reader's electromagnetic field).

Key Features:

Range: RFID tags can be read from a few centimeters to several meters away, depending on the frequency and type of tag.

Data Capacity: Tags can store various amounts of data, from a simple ID number to detailed information about the tagged item.

Durability: RFID tags are typically durable and can withstand harsh environmental conditions.

Applications:

Inventory Management: Tracking goods in warehouses and retail stores to optimize inventory levels and reduce losses.

Access Control: Controlling access to buildings or secure areas using RFID-enabled badges.

Asset Tracking: Monitoring the location and status of assets in industries like healthcare, logistics, and manufacturing.

Advantages:

Automated Identification: Provides quick and accurate identification of objects without manual intervention.

Improved Efficiency: Enhances operational efficiency by automating tracking and inventory processes.

2.Near Field Communication (NFC)

NFC is a short-range wireless communication technology that enables data exchange between devices within a few centimeters. NFC is commonly used in contactless payment systems, access control, and data sharing between devices.

Key Features:

Short Range: Typically operates within a range of 4 centimeters or less.

Ease of Use: Enables simple, tap-based interactions for quick data exchange.

Secure Communication: Supports secure communication protocols, making it suitable for payment and authentication applications.

Applications:

Contactless Payments: Facilitating secure transactions using NFC-enabled cards and mobile devices.

Smartphones: Enabling data sharing, such as contact information or photos, between NFC-enabled devices.

Public Transport: Allowing contactless ticketing and access to public transportation systems.

Advantages:

Convenience: Provides a simple and intuitive way to exchange information and perform transactions.

Security: Offers secure communication protocols to protect sensitive data.

3. Bluetooth

Bluetooth is a wireless technology standard used for exchanging data over short distances using UHF radio waves. It is widely used in personal devices, IoT applications, and smart home devices.

Key Features:

Range: Typically operates within a range of up to 100 meters, depending on the device and environment.

Low Power Consumption: Designed to consume minimal power, making it suitable for battery-operated devices.

Data Rate: Provides moderate data transfer rates, suitable for audio streaming, file transfer, and device communication.

Applications:

Wireless Audio Devices: Connecting headphones, speakers, and other audio devices to smartphones and computers.

Wearables: Enabling communication between fitness trackers, smartwatches, and mobile devices.

Home Automation: Connecting smart home devices like lights, locks, and thermostats.

Advantages:

Ubiquity: Widely supported by a vast array of consumer electronics and IoT devices.

Low Power: Suitable for applications requiring low power consumption, such as wearables and sensors.

4. Wi-Fi

Wi-Fi is a wireless networking technology that uses radio waves to provide high-speed internet and network connections. It is commonly used in homes, offices, and public spaces to connect devices to the internet.

Key Features:

Range: Typically covers a range of up to 100 meters indoors and up to 300 meters outdoors.

High Data Rate: Supports high data transfer rates, suitable for streaming, gaming, and large file transfers.

Network Connectivity: Allows multiple devices to connect to a local area network (LAN) and the internet.

Applications:

Home and Office Networking: Providing internet access and network connectivity to devices like computers, smartphones, and smart TVs.

Public Wi-Fi: Offering internet access in public places like cafes, airports, and hotels.

IoT Devices: Connecting smart home devices, security cameras, and other IoT devices to the network.

Advantages:

High Speed: Supports high-speed data transfer for demanding applications like video streaming and online gaming.

Widespread Adoption: Widely used and supported by numerous devices and applications.

5. Zigbee

Zigbee is a low-power, low-data-rate wireless communication protocol designed for IoT applications. It is particularly well-suited for creating mesh networks, where devices communicate with each other to extend the network range.

Key Features:

Low Power Consumption: Designed to consume minimal power, extending battery life for connected devices.

Mesh Networking: Supports mesh networking, enabling devices to relay data to each other and extend the network's range.

Scalability: Can support large networks with many devices.

Applications:

Home Automation: Connecting smart home devices like lights, locks, and thermostats.

Industrial Automation: Enabling wireless communication in industrial settings for monitoring and control.

Smart Agriculture: Connecting sensors and devices for precision farming and environmental monitoring.

Advantages:

Energy Efficiency: Optimized for low power consumption, making it ideal for battery-operated devices.

Mesh Networking: Enhances network reliability and coverage through mesh networking.

6. LoRaWAN (Long Range Wide Area Network)

LoRaWAN is a low-power, wide-area networking protocol designed for IoT applications. It enables long-range communication between IoT devices and gateways, making it suitable for applications that require extended coverage.

Key Features:

Long Range: Supports communication ranges of up to 15 kilometers in rural areas and several kilometers in urban environments.

Low Power Consumption: Designed for low power consumption, allowing devices to operate for years on battery power.

Scalability: Supports large networks with thousands of devices.

Applications:

Smart Cities: Connecting sensors and devices for applications like smart lighting, waste management, and environmental monitoring.

Agriculture: Enabling remote monitoring of soil conditions, weather, and crop health.

Asset Tracking: Providing long-range tracking of assets and inventory in logistics and supply chain management.

Advantages:

Extended Coverage: Provides long-range communication, ideal for wide-area applications.

Battery Life: Optimized for low power consumption, ensuring long battery life for connected devices.

Connectivity technologies such as RFID, NFC, Bluetooth, Wi-Fi, Zigbee, and LoRaWAN are essential components of the IoT ecosystem, each offering unique features and advantages for specific applications. RFID and NFC are ideal for short-range identification and communication, while Bluetooth and Wi-Fi provide higher data rates for personal and home networking. Zigbee and LoRaWAN are well-suited for low-power, long-range applications in industrial, agricultural, and smart city settings. By understanding the capabilities and benefits of these connectivity technologies, organizations can choose the right solutions to meet their specific IoT needs and drive innovation across various domains.

Fog Computing and Edge Computing

Fog computing and edge computing are two complementary paradigms in the field of distributed computing, both aiming to extend cloud computing capabilities closer to the source of data generation. These approaches address latency, bandwidth, and security issues by processing data locally, near the data source, rather than relying solely on centralized cloud data centers. This section explores the definitions, key features, benefits, applications, and distinctions between fog computing and edge computing.

1.Fog Computing

Fog computing, also known as fog networking or fogging, is an architecture that distributes computing, storage, and networking resources closer to the data sources. It extends the cloud's capabilities to the edge of the network, enabling localized processing and storage. This reduces the amount of data sent to the cloud, minimizes latency, and improves response times.

Key Features:

Decentralized Processing: Distributes data processing across multiple nodes, such as routers, gateways, and edge devices, rather than relying on a central cloud.

Proximity to Data Source: Places computing resources closer to where data is generated, reducing latency and bandwidth usage.

Scalability: Supports large-scale deployments by distributing workloads across a network of fog nodes.

Interoperability: Integrates with various IoT devices and platforms, providing seamless data processing and communication.

Benefits:

Reduced Latency: By processing data closer to the source, fog computing minimizes the time it takes to analyze and act on data.

Bandwidth Efficiency: Reduces the amount of data transmitted to the cloud, saving bandwidth and lowering costs.

Enhanced Security: Data can be processed locally, reducing the exposure to potential security threats during transmission.

Scalability and Flexibility: Can easily scale to accommodate a growing number of devices and data sources.

Applications:

Smart Cities: Enhances traffic management, public safety, and environmental monitoring by processing data locally.

Industrial IoT: Improves efficiency and response times in manufacturing and automation by processing sensor data on-site.
Healthcare: Enables real-time patient monitoring and medical data analysis at the point of care.
Retail: Supports local processing of data from in-store sensors and cameras for inventory management and customer insights.

2.Edge Computing

Edge computing is a distributed computing model that brings computation and data storage closer to the location where it is needed, improving response times and saving bandwidth. Edge computing places computing resources at the edge of the network, such as on IoT devices, gateways, or local servers, rather than in a centralized cloud.

Key Features:

Local Processing: Performs data processing at or near the data source, reducing the need to send data to a central location.
Low Latency: Delivers real-time processing and quick responses by minimizing the distance data needs to travel.
Autonomy: Edge devices can operate independently, even when disconnected from the central cloud or network.
Resource Efficiency: Utilizes local computing resources, which can be more efficient and cost-effective for certain tasks.

Benefits:

Immediate Insights: Provides real-time data analysis and decision-making capabilities, essential for time-sensitive applications.
Reduced Bandwidth Usage: Lowers the volume of data transmitted to the cloud, saving bandwidth and reducing costs.
Enhanced Reliability: Ensures continuous operation and local processing even if the connection to the central cloud is lost.
Security and Privacy: Keeps sensitive data closer to its source, enhancing security and privacy controls.

Applications:

Autonomous Vehicles: Processes data from sensors and cameras in real-time for navigation and safety features.
Smart Homes: Manages local processing for devices like smart thermostats, security systems, and home automation hubs.
Healthcare Devices: Supports real-time data analysis for wearables and medical devices, enabling immediate health interventions.
Remote Monitoring: Facilitates local data processing for remote monitoring systems in agriculture, energy, and environmental sectors.

3.Comparison Between Fog Computing and Edge Computing

Architecture:

Fog Computing: Distributes computing resources across a network of nodes, including routers, gateways, and local servers, extending cloud capabilities closer to the edge.

Edge Computing: Focuses on processing data directly on the devices or near the data source, such as IoT devices, sensors, or local servers.

Processing Location:

Fog Computing: Processes data at intermediate nodes between the cloud and the edge, offering a hierarchical approach to data management.

Edge Computing: Processes data at or near the data source, providing immediate local processing and decision-making.

Use Cases:

Fog Computing: Ideal for applications requiring data aggregation and processing across multiple nodes, such as smart cities and industrial automation.

Edge Computing: Suitable for applications needing real-time data processing and low latency, such as autonomous vehicles and smart homes.

Scalability:

Fog Computing: Scales by adding more fog nodes to the network, accommodating large-scale and geographically dispersed deployments.

Edge Computing: Scales by deploying additional edge devices, each capable of local processing and storage.

Latency:

Fog Computing: Offers low latency by reducing the distance data needs to travel, but may still involve multiple hops.

Edge Computing: Provides the lowest latency by processing data directly at the source, ensuring immediate responses.

Fog computing and edge computing are transformative technologies that enhance the capabilities of cloud computing by bringing data processing and storage closer to the data source. Fog computing distributes resources across a network of nodes, providing a scalable and flexible solution for applications like smart cities and industrial IoT. Edge computing focuses on local processing, offering real-time insights and low latency for applications such as autonomous vehicles and smart homes. Both paradigms play a crucial role in the IoT ecosystem, addressing challenges related to latency, bandwidth, and security, and enabling the development of innovative, efficient, and reliable applications. By understanding the distinctions and synergies between fog and edge computing, organizations can leverage these technologies to optimize their operations and drive digital transformation.

IoT Case Studies (Smart Homes, Smart Cities, Connected Vehicles, Industrial IoT Applications)

The Internet of Things (IoT) is transforming various sectors by enabling smarter, more efficient, and connected systems. This section explores real-world IoT case studies across four key areas: Smart Homes, Smart Cities, Connected Vehicles, and Industrial IoT Applications. These case studies highlight the practical applications, benefits, and impact of IoT technologies.

1. Smart Homes

Smart homes use IoT devices to automate and enhance the management of household systems and appliances. These systems can include lighting, heating, security, entertainment, and more, all controlled via a central hub or smartphone app.

Case Study: Nest Smart Thermostat

Nest, a subsidiary of Google, developed a smart thermostat that learns the user's schedule and preferences to optimize heating and cooling. The device connects to the home Wi-Fi network and can be controlled remotely via a mobile app.

Key Features:

Learning Algorithm: Automatically adjusts temperature settings based on user behavior and preferences.
Energy Savings: Provides insights into energy usage and suggests ways to reduce consumption.
Remote Access: Allows users to control the thermostat from anywhere using a smartphone.
Integration: Compatible with other smart home devices and platforms, such as Google Assistant and Amazon Alexa.

Benefits:

Convenience: Automates climate control, reducing the need for manual adjustments.
Energy Efficiency: Helps users save on energy bills by optimizing heating and cooling.
Enhanced Comfort: Maintains optimal temperature settings tailored to user preferences.
Easy Installation: Simple setup process, making it accessible to a wide range of users.

2. Smart Cities

Smart cities leverage IoT technologies to improve urban infrastructure, enhance public services, and create sustainable environments. IoT applications in smart cities aim to optimize resource use, reduce costs, and improve the quality of life for residents.

Case Study: Barcelona Smart City Initiative

Barcelona has implemented a comprehensive smart city initiative that integrates various IoT solutions to enhance urban living. The city uses IoT technologies for smart parking, waste management, lighting, and environmental monitoring.

Key Features:

Smart Parking: Sensors detect available parking spaces and guide drivers to them via a mobile app, reducing traffic congestion.

Smart Lighting: Streetlights equipped with sensors adjust brightness based on ambient light and pedestrian activity, saving energy.

Waste Management: Smart bins monitor waste levels and optimize collection routes, reducing operational costs and environmental impact.

Environmental Monitoring: Sensors track air quality, noise levels, and weather conditions to provide real-time data for urban planning.

Benefits:

Traffic Reduction: Decreases traffic congestion and emissions by optimizing parking and transportation.

Energy Savings: Reduces energy consumption through intelligent lighting and efficient waste management.

Improved Services: Enhances public services by using data-driven insights for better decision-making.

Sustainability: Promotes environmental sustainability through efficient resource management.

3. Connected Vehicles

Connected vehicles use IoT technologies to communicate with other vehicles, infrastructure, and the cloud. This connectivity enhances safety, efficiency, and the overall driving experience by providing real-time data and automated functions.

Case Study: Tesla Autopilot

Overview: Tesla's Autopilot is an advanced driver-assistance system (ADAS) that uses IoT technologies, including sensors, cameras, and radar, to enable semi-autonomous driving. The system receives software updates over the air (OTA) to continuously improve its capabilities.

Key Features:

Autonomous Driving: Supports features like lane keeping, adaptive cruise control, and automated lane changes.

Over-the-Air Updates: Continuously improves functionality and safety with regular software updates.

Data Collection: Collects and analyses data from the vehicle's sensors to enhance driving algorithms.

Remote Monitoring: Allows owners to monitor and control their vehicles via the Tesla mobile app.

Benefits:

Enhanced Safety: Reduces the risk of accidents through advanced driver-assistance features.

Convenience: Automates driving tasks, reducing driver fatigue and stress.

Continuous Improvement: Regular updates ensure the system stays up-to-date with the latest advancements.

User Control: Provides remote access and monitoring capabilities for vehicle management.

4. Industrial IoT Applications

Industrial IoT (IIoT) involves the use of IoT technologies in industrial sectors to enhance operational efficiency, productivity, and safety. IIoT connects machines, sensors, and devices to collect and analyse data for better decision-making and automation.

Case Study: GE Predix Platform

Overview: GE's Predix is an industrial IoT platform designed to connect machines and collect data for predictive maintenance and operational optimization. The platform serves various industries, including manufacturing, energy, and transportation.

Key Features:

Predictive Maintenance: Uses data analytics to predict equipment failures and schedule maintenance before breakdowns occur.

Operational Optimization: Analyses data to optimize processes and improve efficiency.

Asset Performance Management: Monitors the performance of industrial assets in real-time to identify areas for improvement.

Scalability: Supports large-scale industrial deployments with extensive data collection and processing capabilities.

Benefits:

Reduced Downtime: Minimizes unplanned downtime through predictive maintenance.

Increased Efficiency: Optimizes industrial processes, leading to cost savings and improved productivity.

Enhanced Safety: Monitors equipment and operations to ensure safety standards are met.

Data-Driven Insights: Provides actionable insights for better decision-making and strategic planning.

These IoT case studies in Smart Homes, Smart Cities, Connected Vehicles, and Industrial IoT Applications demonstrate the transformative potential of IoT technologies across various sectors. By leveraging IoT solutions, organizations can enhance efficiency, improve user experiences, and drive innovation. The successful implementation of IoT projects, as illustrated in these case studies, highlights the significant benefits of IoT in creating smarter, more connected, and more sustainable systems.

Summary

Mobile Cloud Computing (MCC): Combines mobile and cloud computing for enhanced device capabilities. Key features: resource augmentation, scalability, data management, mobility. Benefits: extended battery life, enhanced performance, flexibility, cost efficiency. Applications: mobile gaming, mHealth, mCommerce, mLearning. Challenges: connectivity, security, latency.

Automatic Cloud Computing (ACC): Uses automation for cloud resource management. Key features: automated provisioning, self-healing, resource optimization, scalability. Benefits: operational efficiency, cost savings, enhanced reliability, agility. Applications: DevOps, IT operations, disaster recovery, resource management. Challenges: complexity, security risks, algorithm dependency.

Internet Protocol Television (IPTV): TV content over IP networks. Key features: on-demand content, live streaming, interactive services, multi-device support. Benefits: scalability, cost efficiency, flexibility, enhanced user experience. Applications: residential TV, corporate communications, education, hospitality. Challenges: bandwidth, content licensing, security.

Energy-Aware Cloud Computing: Optimizes energy use in data centers. Key features: dynamic resource allocation, energy-efficient hardware, virtualization, renewable energy. Benefits: cost savings, reduced environmental impact, regulatory compliance, enhanced efficiency. Applications: green data centers, smart grids, IoT, big data. Challenges: initial costs, complexity, performance trade-offs.

Distributed Cloud Computing: Cloud services across multiple locations. Key features: global distribution, centralized management, scalability, redundancy. Benefits: reduced latency, enhanced performance, high availability, cost efficiency. Applications: CDNs, global SaaS, financial services, e-commerce. Challenges: management complexity, data security, coordination latency.

Edge Computing: Local data processing near the source. Key features: local processing, low latency, autonomy, resource efficiency. Benefits: immediate insights, reduced bandwidth, enhanced security, improved reliability. Applications: autonomous vehicles, smart homes, healthcare devices, remote monitoring. Challenges: management complexity, security risks, data consistency.

Fog Computing vs. Edge Computing: Fog computing extends cloud capabilities to network nodes, offering decentralized processing and scalability. Edge computing focuses on local processing at data sources, providing ultra-low latency and real-time insights. Both improve latency, bandwidth, and security for IoT applications.

IoT Case Studies:

Smart Homes (Nest Thermostat): Automated climate control, energy savings, remote access, integration.

Smart Cities (Barcelona): Smart parking, lighting, waste management, environmental monitoring, improved public services.

Connected Vehicles (Tesla Autopilot): Autonomous driving, OTA updates, data collection, remote monitoring, enhanced safety.

Industrial IoT (GE Predix): Predictive maintenance, operational optimization, asset performance management, reduced downtime, increased efficiency.

Glossary

Consumer IoT: Devices and applications for convenience and automation in daily life, including smart homes, wearables, and smart appliances.

Industrial IoT (IIoT): Enhances efficiency and safety in industrial sectors with smart factories, predictive maintenance, and supply chain management.

Healthcare IoT: Connected devices for patient monitoring, disease management, and improved healthcare delivery, such as remote patient monitoring and smart medical devices.

Smart Cities: Uses IoT to improve urban infrastructure and public services, including smart transportation, environmental monitoring, and smart grids.

Connectivity Technologies: Essential for IoT, including RFID for tracking, NFC for short-range communication, Bluetooth for personal devices, Wi-Fi for high-speed connections, and Zigbee for low-power applications.

Scalability: IoT systems must handle increasing devices and data volumes, ensuring they can expand without compromising performance.

Security: Critical for IoT, requiring encryption, authentication, and regular updates to protect against cyberattacks and ensure data privacy.

Real-Time Processing: Necessary for applications like autonomous vehicles and healthcare monitoring, allowing immediate data insights and responses.

Edge and Fog Computing: Brings data processing closer to the source, reducing latency and improving response times for applications like smart cities and industrial IoT.

Exercise

Exercise 1 – MCQ

Which of the following is an example of an IoT connectivity technology used for short-range communication?

Wi-Fi

NFC

Ethernet

LTE

What term describes extending cloud capabilities closer to IoT devices to reduce latency and bandwidth use?

Cloud Computing

Fog Computing

Grid Computing

Distributed Computing

Exercise 2 – True/ False

RFID and NFC are both types of connectivity technologies used in IoT for short-range communication.

Fog computing processes data in a centralized cloud to manage IoT devices efficiently.

Exercise 3 – Fill in the blanks

____________ is a short-range wireless communication technology commonly used for contactless payments and data sharing between devices within a few centimeters.

____________ is an architecture that distributes computing, storage, and networking resources closer to the data sources, often used to reduce latency and improve response times in IoT applications.

Exercise 4 – One-Word

Which IoT connectivity technology is commonly used for short-range communication?

What term is used for extending cloud capabilities closer to the data source in IoT?

Exercise 5 – Small answer

What are the key characteristics that differentiate Consumer IoT from Industrial IoT (IIoT)?

How does RFID technology contribute to inventory management in IoT applications?

Exercise 6 – Long answer

Discuss the various categories of IoT and provide examples of how each category is utilized in real-world applications.

Explain how IoT and Cloud Computing converge to enhance the capabilities of smart cities, focusing on connectivity technologies and data processing models like Fog and Edge Computing.

Answer

Exercise 1 – MCQ

Ans: 1 b, 2 b.

Exercise 2 – True/False

Ans: 1 True, 2 False.

Exercise 3 – Fill in The Blanks

Ans: 1NFC (Near Field Communication), 2 Fog Computing.

Exercise 4 – One-Word

Ans: 1 NFC, 2 Edge Computing.

Online Resources

1. **True/False Practice Paper :** **https://forms.gle/nYErWF9rCtiYYPPs6**

QR Code

2. **True/False Video Link :**

https://www.youtube.com/playlist?list=PLzlh 31VWEFrIdZe3TCyEwYKUXlymybDS

QR Code

3. **One Word Practice Paper :** **https://forms.gle/BNTnshy4NGv5wShn6**

QR Code

4. **One Word Video Link :**

https://www.youtube.com/playlist?list=PLzlh 31VWEFoJ3LBMfwQAqJ sL7aJH0-F

QR Code

ADDITIONAL RESOURCES

https://www.youtube.com/playlist?list=PLzlh 31VWEFpK7TLTz5Sa8mEhbkvrdyqk

QR Code:

www.ingramcontent.com/pod-product-compliance
Lightning Source LLC
Chambersburg PA
CBHW061218240926
51846CB00006B/1265
9789369915989